Where Do Broken Hearts Go?

Ron Elliott
4220 Perry Ave. NE
Bremerton, WA 98310

Where Do Broken Hearts Go?

An Integrative, Participational Theology of Grief

W. ROSS HASTINGS

FOREWORD BY
Dr. Judith McBride, Psychiatrist

CASCADE *Books* · Eugene, Oregon

WHERE DO BROKEN HEARTS GO?
An Integrative, Participational Theology of Grief

Cascade Books
An Imprint of Wipf and Stock Publishers
199 W. 8th Ave., Suite 3
Eugene, OR 97401

www.wipfandstock.com

PAPERBACK ISBN: 978-1-4982-7847-8
HARDCOVER ISBN: 978-1-4982-7849-2
EBOOK ISBN: 978-1-4982-7848-5

Cataloguing-in-Publication data:

Names: Hastings, W. Ross.
Title: Where do broken hearts go? : an integrative, participational theology of grief / W. Ross Hastings.
Description: Eugene, OR: Cascade Books, 2016 | Includes bibliographical references and index.
Identifiers: ISBN 978-1-4982-7847-8 (paperback) | ISBN 978-1-4982-7849-2 (hardcover) | ISBN 978-1-4982-7848-5 (ebook)
Subjects: LCSH:1. Grief—Religious aspects—Christianity. 2. Bereavement—Religious aspects—Christianity. 3. Loss (Psychology)—Religious aspects—Christianity. 4. Consolation—Religious aspects—Christianity. I. McBride, Judith. II. Title.
Classification: BV4460.6 H37 2016 (print) | BV4460.6 (ebook)

Manufactured in the U.S.A.   JUNE 23, 2016

Dedicated to
Willie and Betty Hastings

Table of Contents

Foreword

Why another book to add to the vast amount of literature addressing the subject of death and dying? Many theoretical works as well as personal narrative accounts of the dying process are readily available.

In *Where Do Broken Hearts Go?* Dr. Hastings is clear in stating that this is not one more self-help guide, and it isn't. There are no formulas for us to apply to our own or others' grief. Through his extensive theological training and experience in ministry, together with psychological insights into his own life, the author addresses a glaring gap in the faith-based literature on grief and loss. He offers us a grounded and compelling account of the nature of bereavement. In doing so he makes a valuable contribution to the Christian community, laity and clergy alike.

Life inevitably presents us with painful and complicated losses. Our culture of individualism and its pervasive message of self-reliance is not adequate to explain our universal yet unique experiences of grief. In order to understand the profound effects of loss it is important that we be brought back to the central truth that as human beings we are inextricably embedded in relationship.

The substantively verified psychological avenue of enquiry that best resonates with this truth is attachment theory. The author unpacks this process of bonding accurately and coherently, yet he does not leave us with theory alone. He roots this knowledge in lived descriptions of his own responses and emotions.

Psychotherapy has been described as taking place in the "relational space" between the therapist and patient. While this is true, it is equally true to say that there is an inescapable relational space where bonding and attachment occurs for every one of us; the channel through which love and healing, pain and grief flow. This "space" is not only in individual relationships but also describes our place in community. The author draws our attention to this interpersonal space, through conversation between theology and psychological theories as seen through the lens of loss.

From this integrative perspective the writer further probes what it means to be made in the image of God. He systematically and articulately opens out our God-given relationality as mirrored in the Trinity. The truth that love and communication are at the center of the Trinity is fundamental to our understanding of ourselves individually and corporately. We discover that relationship with others is not an add-on to life for which we make preparation in solitude. Rather it is essential to our nature, shaping and forming us into the persons we are. It is the air we breathe, the oxygen that sustains us both physically and spiritually.

The inevitability of relationship becomes clear when we reflect on our temporal and spiritual journey through life. Our physical life begins at conception in the context of relationship. We are received into relationship at birth, we mature physically and psychologically, discovering "who we are" in the context of relationship. We bear in our bodies and minds, the health as well as the hurt and wounds of relationship.

In our spiritual journey as Christ's disciples we are brought to faith and are baptized into a living relationship with the Trinity. We also enter into the mystery of being members of the body of Christ where we live in fellowship within the network of relationships that is the family of God. What is being described here is communion, a word that captures a sense of mystery as we participate with one another in the life of Christ.

As Christians, we understand death to be the gateway into a fuller communion in the life and love of God, an entry into our eternal home. As our physical life ends, we and those we love experience the final rupture in the bonds of relationship and its accompanying grief. As the author describes the overwhelming impact of his loss on his sense of self and home and belonging, he illustrates in a compelling way the reality, depth, and cost of our relational attachments.

Where Do Broken Hearts Go? brings the theory of attachment and loss into dialogue with the foundational truths of trinitarian theology and the author's own profound experiences of grief and loss. In so doing Dr. Hastings has achieved a masterful weaving of all three elements in an engaging and informative study. This three-way conversation is bigger than the sum of its parts, as it lays a foundation of understanding that informs not only our own personal journeys but also is helpful as we seek to accompany others in the face of their sorrows.

Having known Dr. Hastings over the years it is my great privilege to recommend this most thoughtful and engaging book.

Judith McBride MD, FRCP
Bowen Island, BC
October 2015

Preface

"He heals the brokenhearted and binds up their wounds. He determines the number of the stars and calls them each by name." (Ps 147:3–4, NIV)

ASTRONOMERS ESTIMATE THAT THERE are roughly 70 billion trillion (7 x 10^{22}) stars in the observable universe. This declaration by the Psalmist that God knows each of them by name, though written in pre-Hubble telescopic times, expresses the author's awareness of the immensity and majesty of God. However, astronomy was subservient to the main point of this declaration. Its juxtaposition with the previous verse is what is so stunning—not only because it portrays a God who is both immense and transcendent on the one hand, and closely immanent on the other. It seems to me the Psalmist is letting the exilic community to whom this is written know that the Lord knew *their* names, and that their brokenheartedness and the wounds of *each* of them were known and could be healed by him. This is a clear revelation of a personal God, who is personal in his compassionate action towards human persons.

In a world of population explosion and urbanized anonymity, a world in which it can feel like each of us is merely a number, this *personalist* understanding is true comfort. He knows your name. He knows mine. He knows the wounds I have received in life, and as an all-knowing, loving Father, he knows how to work towards the mending of our broken hearts.

This is not to validate the individualism that runs rife in our Western culture. Me-centered self-determination is not what this entails. Counter to both individualism and its polar opposite, collectivism, the biblical view of humans is that they are persons which are by definition, persons-in-community, echoing in a small way the Trinity of persons-in-communion.

The good news of the Christian gospel is that this personal God has revealed himself as open for personal relations with us. He has reached out to us in real history through the Scriptures, but he has done so supremely by sending his Son to become one with us, to suffer with us, to die for our sins, and to carry us and our pain into the inner life of God. God has also given us his Holy Spirit so that in real time in our history, we can be awakened to life, and regenerated so we have the capacity to receive the salvation and comfort of Christ in our own personal history, in real time. The God who knows our name most often ministers healing to us in community, in the life of the church, and in counseling with skilled persons—and through books written by others.

This is a book born out of the experience of the comfort of the triune God in a loss I never could have imagined. Cancer and death happen to other people, not to me, I had thought, mostly subconsciously. This immersion into the depth of disease and death was an immersion into humanity, into its fallen, broken, dying state, into the desolation of the loss of the emotional center of my life. But above all, in the economy of God's grace, it has been a fresh immersion into him. In the depths and in the comfort. Recovery is always a process, and it is ongoing. In this book I tell my story merely because I hope it will be a means for you to find comfort in a God who is there, there for *you*, there to comfort, there to redeem even the worst of losses. There, never to let you go. There because you matter even more than named stars.

What follows in this book, then, is an integrative and participational approach in which we have tried to bring the best insights of the psychology of grief into conversation with the insights of first-order Christian theology about the triune God, about the human person and psyche. Its aim is to offer the comfort of the God who is there, there in Christ and by the Spirit, there for each one of us as our Father.

Acknowledgements

I can never express adequately my love for and appreciation of the person whose loss gave rise to the writing of this book. My wife Sharon (nee Rae) Hastings, originally from Prestwick, Scotland, died on September 23, 2008 after a twenty-one-month battle with cancer. A little of the story of our lives together and of her loss is contained herein. The fact that God gifted me with the love and companionship of another remarkable woman three years later is a tribute to his amazing and undeserved grace. I am equally inadequate to express my love for Tammy Carrillo and my appreciation for the sacrifices she has made to allow me time and space to write this book. I am very grateful also for editorial suggestions made by Dr. Judith McBride, psychiatrist extraordinaire, whose wise and gentle counsel over many years brought shalom to my soul, increasing my capacity for worshiping God and relating intimately and pastorally to human persons. Dr. McBride looked after me for years in my struggle with depression, and as a person of deep faith, was much more than a brilliant, insightful therapist. She became for me a spiritual director, helping me discern the movements of my soul and the movements of God in my soul. The counsel also of Dr. Peter Kyne, a psychiatrist of Orthodox faith, led to a good psychiatric care but also to deep encounter with God in ways that the Orthodox heritage encourages so well. I am thankful also for the support of Sharon's family, John and Carole Rae, and Margaret and Stuart Fordham, and her devoted friends, Isobel Davidson, Linda Gilbert, Susan Bates, Jean Daly, Tracey Dickie, Pat Jones, and Jeanette McTaggart, who carried her to the end. I am grateful also for true friends who were present to me in my loss. One whose conversations have always left me with a deepened passion for God is Dr. Ivan Stewart, palliative physician, with whom I have enjoyed deep friendship for thirty years. His friendship is the kind that flies 3,000 miles when depressions hit or when remissions are no more. Another friend who always helped

xv

me think straight and refueled my vision for the kingdom of God was Len Hordyk, an elder, a top-flight Vancouver CEO, and the father of six. Sadly, he died of cancer two years ago. My friends on the pastoral staff of Peace Portal Alliance Church in White Rock—Scott Dickie, Phil Vanderveen, Jon Imbeau, and Jim Postlewaite—have also been a huge source of strength to me. The friendship of Dr. Lourens Perold, who cared unstintingly, above and beyond, has also been an immeasurable strength. The wise and compassionate listening of Rod Wilson was significant, as was the deeply spiritual and Christocentric reflection of Darrell Johnson. Others on the faculty at Regent College showed great compassion and offered much wisdom.

In the preparation of this book, my teaching assistants at Regent College, Brittany McComb, Kevin Greenlee, and Meredith Cochran have also provided very helpful bibliographic and editorial assistance for which I am profoundly thankful. I extend thanks also to Lindsey G. Robertson, who was very helpful in providing recommended resources and readings in the psychology of grief area. I am also very thankful to Kathy Gillin for her superb editorial work on this manuscript, which has rendered it much more readable and accessible. I am very grateful also for the excellent editorial work of Robin Parry of Cascade Books. I must express also my indebtedness to the board and faculty of Regent College. Not only did the College extend grace to me by granting me compassionate leave immediately following the loss of my wife, but many in this community of scholars extended personal grace to me. The extent to which the stimulating intellectual environment at Regent has engendered my own personal growth is incalculable. A few rich conversations on the content of this book with Jim Houston provide but one example.

List of Abbreviations

CD: Karl Barth, *Church Dogmatics*. 14 volumes. Edited
           by G. W. Bromiley and T. F. Torrance. 2nd ed.
           Edinburgh: T. & T. Clark, 1936–77.

ESV: The Holy Bible, English Standard Version,
           Copyright © 2001 by Crossway. All Rights Reserved.

NIV: The Holy Bible, New International Version,
           Copyright © 1973, 1978, 1984, 2011 by International
           Bible Society (Biblica). All Rights Reserved. All
           Scripture quotations, unless otherwise stated, are taken
           from this version of the Holy Bible.

Introduction

THIS MAY BE HARD to believe, but my inspiration for persevering in writing on the subject of loss and grief came partly from an experience I had watching a One Direction concert in Vancouver. Yes, it's pop culture and I am certain there is a wide diversity of opinion about its quality, even within that category. I went for the sake of a younger member of the family, as one does.

After an opening song that just about burst my eardrums, I was observing the crowd and listening to the mellower tunes when suddenly they started singing their song, "Where do broken hearts go?" For reasons beyond the immediate circumstances, I began to be deeply moved. I was broken for most of the song and well after. I experienced a burst of fresh grief for the loss of my wife, who never would have come to a noisy event like this, but who would have been interested to hear about it afterwards. But my grief went beyond that.

I looked down from our seats in the rafters at this crowd of mainly children, teenagers, and young adults, and I just seemed to sense their pain, present and future. The words "where do broken hearts go?" reverberated in my head and heart, and with them the feeling of abandonment that results from a hard reality: for many, there seems to be precisely nowhere for broken hearts to go. I remember thinking also that the only One to whom broken hearts can go—and the church that is his community for mending hearts, and the spiritual practices that God has given to receive his healing presence—are lost to many in this generation with its multitudinous social media distractions and its fantasy world of pop idols, its tendency to drown sorrows rather than face them, to compensate and self-medicate with binge drinking and the drugs so readily available. The amount of loss being endured from physically and emotionally absent parents, and from broken marriages in this achievement-oriented boomer generation, seemed to seep into my own soul. The possibility—no, the probability—that this will have a multiplied effect in the coming generation brought no comfort. When hearts break from the loss of friendships so valued in this culture, where do they go? When we lose someone who has become our primary attachment in place of absent parents, people like grandparents, siblings, aunts or uncles, or friends, where do we go with our broken hearts? When we lose pets that may have become the primary attachment that has saved us from a chaotic and troubled home life, where do we go? When hearts break from losses like divorce and death from cancer, where do they go?

Also on my heart that night of watching screaming fans fawn over four ordinary humans were communities far beyond the Western community of entitlement and wealth. Communities in Syria and Iraq, for whom loss through death is a daily occurrence because of ongoing war. Communities in various countries of Africa, where life expectancy is much lower than in North America, where medical help is scarce and so parents and children die of treatable diseases—and untreatable diseases too. Where do these broken hearts go? I saw an image in my mind of a little boy running with hands outstretched, tears streaming down his cheeks, looking around with terror in his eyes, unable to land, unable to find his parents, who had just been shot in a senseless war. Where do these broken hearts go?

If I don't have some kind of an answer to that question, I may as well throw away my theology books and look for another career. At the heart of the Christian gospel is a loving triune God to whom we *can* go; specifically, a Father of compassion who embraces us, a Son who entered into the heart of our pain and brokenness, who gathers up our sorrows and presents them to the Father, and at the same time, comes to us by his presence within and among us in the Holy Spirit, the Comforter.

In this book, we will look closely at this theology of comfort. Where do broken hearts go? To the *Triune God*, Father, Son, and Holy Spirit. In our opening section, we will explore what we can and cannot know about loss and grief. We will speak of the revelation of this triune God, and of an understanding of personhood that is derived from who we are as image-bearers of the Triune God. Then as we discuss the meaning of grief, we will use a trinitarian paradigm, that of grief as "grief-sharing." We will be God-oriented in evaluating contemporary wisdom about grief. In chapter 7, we will consider explicitly the comforting heart of the Triune God.

But the question naturally follows: how do we go to the Father? Receiving comfort in our grief could sound like dry theology. The truth is that the comforting God not only *is* but *is not* silent. He has provided access to himself in his Son Jesus, through the incarnation; but that Son also indwells his church by the presence of the Holy Spirit. God has in fact come to indwell communities of faith that take on his comforting character. Where do broken hearts go? To the church.

That may sound counterintuitive to many who have experienced the church as anything but a place of comfort. The church isn't perfect. It takes humility to be part of the life of the church, because we aren't perfect either, on this side of the new creation. But for all its faults and failings, the church is still the greatest plan God has for humanity and for its salvation. As a pastor, I have known the faults of the church more intimately than most. It, and everyone in it, is still in the redemption process. Despite this, I have found the church unwaveringly compassionate and a huge source of comfort and support for my family and me during the illness and loss of my wife. I want to argue in the second section of this book that the core essence of church is that it mediates the comfort of God, and I will urge churches to think well, in that regard, about their role in a broken world. Not that we should ignore the righteousness and justice and judgment of God, but this is the heart of the Christian gospel: in Christ—the One who has become one with us and has stood in our place—we are made righteous and we are regenerated to be formed towards justice. Above all, we are adopted sons and daughters of the Father, who reflect his forgiving and comforting character to a broken world.

I have argued elsewhere that every church is missional in its identity, because every true Christian church is indwelt by the God who is by identity missional.[1] A crucial aspect of living into this identity as the missional church, therefore, and of reflecting the missional nature of God, is being oriented *outwards* to the other. The church is to be a community that goes out to the grieving and broken, and that draws others into the heart of the God who is on the lookout for his broken—rebellious, but also wounded—children. Churches that reflect the Father heart of God are havens of refuge and communities of comfort, with specific ministries for the healing of the broken. The very nature of the kingdom of God, which the church inhabits and proclaims, is one of relief from and reversal of the effects of the fall. Jesus describes this in Luke 4, using the messianic language of Isaiah 61:1–2:

> The Spirit of the Lord is on me, because he has anointed me to proclaim good news to the poor. He has sent me to proclaim freedom

1. See Hastings, *Missional God*.

for the prisoners and recovery of sight for the blind, to set the op-
pressed free, to proclaim the year of the Lord's favor.

The opening words of the messianic section of Isaiah's great prophecy
express, with the emphasis of repetition, the heart of the gospel: "Comfort,
comfort my people, says your God" (40:1). This is where people wondering where their broken hearts can go *can* go. Of course, it will be crucial
that when people come to gatherings of the church, there will be acknowl-
edgement of grief, and not just happy clappy praise songs. The fact that 40
percent of the Psalms are lament seems to have escaped the notice of those
who lead worship in our time. The Psalms were the prayer and praise book
of the church in New Testament times and for most of its history. Hymn
writers of the eighteenth century, like Isaac Watts and Charles Wesley, actually had to engage in worship wars to get churches to sing anything but
psalms. The worship wars of this past century led to the introduction of
worship songs that might easily be called "spiritual songs," and it is good
and nourishing when a church has a steady, balanced diet of all three—
psalms, hymns, and spiritual songs. But the point is that psalms contain
lament, and all churches need to give room for lament in their worship.
Walter Brueggeman speaks of lament in the Psalms as "The Formfulness of
Grief." He comments that the structure of the psalms of lament mirror the
stages of grief as outlined by Elizabeth Kübler-Ross.[2] Although the merit
of these "stages" has been qualified in today's understanding of the grief
process, the point remains that we cannot be communities of comfort if we
do not cultivate the practice of lament in the life of the church, including
the God-given vehicle of the Psalms. We will devote two chapters (11–12)
to this theme—*the church*, both gathered and scattered, as the community
where broken hearts go.

Although we are persons *in community*, we are *persons* with irreducible identity. Our experience of sadness and loss and grief is personal and
idiosyncratic. Our experience of the comfort of God is also personal. How
do persons experience comfort? Are there certain spiritual practices that
enable us to process grief well? How does a person go to God directly? And
how does a person ultimately become, through the journey of formation,
a refuge for others—a person to whom broken hearts can go? In the final
chapter, we will consider these personal approaches to grief resolution and
formation as comforted persons who are comforters.

2. See Brueggemann, "Formfulness of Grief."

Just to be clear at the outset: this is *not* a book that describes "seven steps" to the "victorious overcoming of grief." We do not overcome grief. Though it need not overcome us, and though, after a while, we can experience adaptation and even growth through its presence, it never leaves. It may become a scab, and even one day a scar, but the losses that bring us grief will always be there. Just there. And scars are prone to fresh tearing at the most unexpected times,

Rather than offering a self-help book, I want to share this story in the hope that it might make some sense of the journey of loss that every human being will at some point undergo. I want to give permission for mourners to feel what mourners feel, and to draw those who mourn into the comfort of the God of all comfort and—when they are ready—into the change that grief inspires and unfolds. Into the hope that is intrinsic to the Christian faith.

chapter 1

A Grief Shared . . . Introducing the Story

WHAT PROMPTED ME TO write a book on this subject? Though I think that an actual experience of loss is an important qualification for writing on this topic, I did not consider this task because I think *my* grief experiences have been greater than others. People incur losses every day that are more tragic than mine. But perhaps in the relative "ordinariness" of our losses, we can best see the extraordinary nature of death and the deep sorrow it brings.

Nor did I write this book because I wish to engage in emotional strip-tease. My rather shy and private Scottish nature presses me in the opposite direction. Rather, in the spirit of 2 Corinthians 1 (where Paul speaks of the cycle of comfort in loss), we share our stories in the hope that others "*may be comforted with the comfort we ourselves have received*" (2 Cor 1:3–4) from the "*Father of compassion and God of all comfort.*"

The Story of Sharon and Ross

I lost my wife Sharon on September 23, 2008. I was married to her for twenty-seven years. I had seen her when we were just children, when my folks were on furlough in Scotland in 1965–66. Even as a nine-year-old, I remember being impressed by this blond, rosy-cheeked, curly-headed little girl. However, I grew up in Rhodesia (now Zimbabwe) and she grew up in Prestwick. I met her again in Scotland in December 1979, at a series of church conferences, and I preached at a service that she and her dad attended, sitting in the front row. I suspect it must have been my worst sermon ever, because it was hard to concentrate. She was so beautiful.

She quickly struck me as the most open and welcoming person I had ever met. Her care for her wheelchair-bound dad was impressive. She was an intensive care nurse with her feet firmly planted on the ground, as practical as I was theoretical and visionary. And she was deeply committed to Christ. There was no dating then, however, as I was only passing through Scotland on my way to Canada to study chemistry.

I had taken note of her, but I needed to get to studying. Four or five months later, I sent her a friendly letter. I had written and destroyed one a month before sending this, thinking it was too strange to write her. She probably would hardly remember me.

To my great surprise, Sharon answered back quickly with warm and open sentiments. We exchanged letters over the next month, in which Sharon later told me she felt I showed too much caution ("a cawny cratur" [cautious creature] was her Scottish vernacular) and did not move along rapidly enough. At the end of the month, I flew to Scotland for a two-week vacation. We certainly moved along rapidly enough in our relationship then. After four days, I asked her to marry me.

That I asked her to marry me after only four days is one measure of how special she was. She was an ICU nursing sister (charge nurse) by the age of twenty-five, and when I visited her at the Glasgow Royal Infirmary, her matron (the nurse in charge of the sisters)—who was as stern as matrons usually were—commanded me to make sure Sharon worked as a nurse all her days, because Sharon was the best nurse she had ever seen.

I was unable to fulfill that command, because Sharon had firm ideas of her own. From the time we came to Canada in 1983 until the last two years of her life, she did not work as a nurse. Instead, she raised two great kids, Martyn and Heather, whom she dressed meticulously and fed nourishingly. Without doubt, she was the emotional center of our home.

Typical of Scottish people from humble circumstances, Sharon had no time for pretentiousness or snobbery. She could have met the Queen and had a down-to-earth conversation about blackcurrant jam or kids without any fear or deference. Don't get me wrong; she respected authority and loved the royal family. My point is that, in a way I have only rarely seen, Sharon treated everyone as a human person, no less and no more. She had a strong sense of identity. On a number of occasions when I might have been struggling with a "power" person in a church or college, she would say something like this: "I don't know why you give that person space in yir heid (your head). Can you not see how insecure s/he is? You should feel sorry for them, not let them give you such anxiety."

Sharon was not a person who ever desired public leadership or a place up front in church life. She worked behind the scenes in each pastorate we served, and she had a special concern for people who were hurting, especially single parents. Our home was frequently open for hospitality, and she loved to cook. She had a remarkable sense of humor that could disarm the proud and lift the spirits of the humble poor. I received the benefit of both ends of that stick! Watching me trip or stumble if my feet hit a raised segment of pavement sent her into raucous laughter, because—I think—it leveled me out of any pompous expectations I might be harboring. She loved to have fun, and sometimes she did outrageous things—such as get the giggles in church in the front row with a friend, while I was trying to preach—or make comical gestures from our front door when waving goodbye to close friends or family who were leaving our home after a dinner. She was a life-giving person to many, and especially to my kids and to me.

Sharon was diagnosed with cancer in December 2006. I shall never forget the moments when she was diagnosed. A specialist from the Vancouver General Hospital, who happened to be giving a seminar to doctors at Peace Arch Hospital in White Rock where we lived (it turns out he was Scottish and had worked at the same hospital as Sharon), had been called upon to examine her in a tiny room in the emergency department. He had extracted fluid from her abdomen, and it had been sent to the lab upstairs to ascertain whether it contained cancerous cells. I was standing watching him work when suddenly a sharp pain in my chest almost bent me double. When the nurse heard it was chest pain, she took me straight to another room in the emergency department, where I was hooked up for an ECG.

So there was our poor daughter, Heather, in one room with her mom and aware that cancer could be the diagnosis, while her dad lay in another room with a possible heart issue. I felt terrible for her, and I cannot express my gratitude that our friend Tracey Dickie was with her in that moment. At any rate, my heart was fine. I merely had esophageal spasms. I was back in Sharon's room in time to hear the confirmation that she had ovarian cancer, and that it was already stage four. I can never forget her first words to me: "Honey, it's been great being married to you. I will miss you." I wanted to remonstrate and say, "Come on honey, don't be so dramatic. There is hope." But I think she knew what she had before the diagnosis was given. Although she was willing to fight with the best of them, she knew what the outcome would be, and that she didn't have long. We had twenty-one months from that day.

Interestingly, Sharon had called her friend Tammy to be with us to pray that day.

In the season of her illness, Sharon had one period of remission. She worked as a practice nurse during that time in the White Rock Medical Clinic and endeared herself to many patients as well as the staff. In July 2008, our friend Tammy's husband Carlos Carrillo reached the point in his brave struggle with cancer where he entered palliative care. Sharon had come to know Tammy and Carlos over a number of years, not only because he was our dentist and attended a small care group in our home, but because Tammy and Sharon had become friends. Every day when Sharon finished her work at the practice, she walked to the hospital and spent time chatting and comforting and praying with Carlos and Tammy, until he died on August 14, 2008. She would often hold his hand and ask about his early life in Colombia, South America, listen attentively, and then say words of comfort and lift his heart to the throne of God.

She died in the same unit forty days later, on September 23, 2008 at 4:05 AM. She passed away in the presence of two devoted friends, Isobel and Linda, who were singing "How Great Thou Art," and specifically the verse, as she breathed her last, that when Christ would come to take her home, what joy would fill her heart. My greatest regret is that I missed that final moment. My children and I had decided to go home to get some sleep in order to be ready for the next day with her, but I received a phone call shortly after 4:05 AM to let me know she had passed away. I should have known that the rasping noise she was making was a consequence of the fact that her vocal cords were no longer functioning, that this was the "death rattle," but I did not know this until afterwards when it was too late. I have nothing but good to say of the nursing and medical staff of the palliative care unit of the Peace Arch Hospital, as their care was outstanding. Predicting the moment of a person's death is not exact science. It is, as we shall see, a mystery resolved in the providence of God. In the words of a line from the movie *Footloose*, "Death is on its own clock."

I have tried not to let my absence there trouble me too greatly, though that has been hard. About six months after Sharon died, I met a senior palliative care physician at Vancouver General Hospital, Dr. Margaret Cottle, who expressed strongly that I should not let my absence at the moment of her death trouble me and not to give sinister forces opportunity to defeat me at this point. Far more importantly, I was there for Sharon for twenty-seven years of marriage. Even at that, I was not perfect, and wouldn't pretend to be. And believe you me, Sharon would call me on it if I wasn't fully there when she was talking to me ("Are you listenin' tae me?"). Through pain and trial and error I had developed those intimacy skills that men find so difficult, and we had a faithful, fun, and intimate marriage that I am so grateful for. God gifted us with two great kids that we took delight in at every stage of their development, and they were well equipped by Sharon for whatever life may bring them. Sharon was surrounded by love that morning, and we had said our goodbyes a number of times, and I had expressed my love to her again and again, even beyond the time when she could respond with her usual reciprocal "love you too." If there was any other regret, it was the fact that I was so anxious about the emotional wellbeing of everybody else who came to visit during her weeks in palliative care that I sometimes failed to be fully present to Sharon, to our children, and to my own emotions.

When Sharon died, I was in shock even though she'd been in palliative care for three weeks. After seven years (at the completion of this book), the shock is only beginning to thaw out. On the day of the loss, what struck me most was the fact that other people continued to live life, shop at the supermarket, drive their cars out of their driveways as if on some all-important mission . . . as if nothing had changed in the world. I had to go to our nearest supermarket to get something for a meal, and as I watched everybody in the store, I had the overwhelming desire to scream, "What are you people doing? Don't you know that Sharon died today?" The reality is that life does go on as if nothing ever happened. This sentiment has been expressed well by Dietrich von Hildebrand: "I am filled with disgust and emptiness over the rhythm of everyday life that goes relentlessly on—as though nothing had changed, as though I had not lost my precious beloved."[1]

I had no further contact with her friend Tammy for two and a half years. Through a set of interesting circumstances, we began to date and were married just over three years after our losses. One of the graces of marrying someone who has also been bereaved of a spouse is our mutual understanding about it. We have been able to speak of each other's spouses without either feeling threatened, and to weep when we need to weep, without insecurity. Our journeys of grief have been similar in some ways and yet significantly different, illustrating the dual reality of both the common or communal and the idiosyncratic or personal dimensions of grief. I will

1. Neuhaus, *Eternal Pity*, 2.

refer to some personal aspects of the grieving journey in the chapters that follow.

Having introduced the structure of the book, my story, and my motivation for writing it, I want now to share a little more about the need that motivates this book, and to introduce our primary theme or motif for understanding loss and grief.

chapter 2

A Grief Shared . . .
Universally by Humanity, and with Divinity

A SIGNIFICANT REASON FOR addressing the issue of grief relates to its universality. Humanity's need for help in this area is incalculable, and so all reasonable efforts are valuable. Grief is the multi-dimensional response to the loss of a loved one or relationship through death or divorce, or to the loss of deep friendships, which sometimes we lose through death, and sometimes we lose through misunderstandings and unresolved conflict, or even a geographical move. Attachment theory suggests that our primary attachments from infancy can be other than to parents, especially when bonding to parents is disrupted. Thus primary attachment can be with a sibling, a grandparent, an aunt or uncle, a neighbor, or a family pet that has been a haven of unconditional love and security in the midst of chaos in a dysfunctional home. These attachments can have profound impact when lost. Even the loss of a job or a home or financial security brings with it a grief. Losses may be physical (such as the concrete loss of a spouse or child or parent or friend) or abstract, relating to one's social interactions. The term "bereavement," though sometimes used interchangeably with "grief," describes the actual loss; grief is our reaction to that loss. Some experts in grief counseling emphasize grief's multi-dimensional nature; that is, its physical, cognitive, social, behavioral, spiritual, and philosophical aspects, along with its emotional or affective qualities. Other experts believe that the focus should be mostly on the emotional suffering.[1]

People who have undergone loss don't need to be convinced about why they might benefit from a book on grief. Many of us, and I was one of them, have a belief that is at some level triumphalistic and aloof: death happens to *other* people. We stay aloof from others in this way until death draws us down with a bump into humanity. I had not lost anyone in my immediate family when I lost my wife. Before that, if I am honest, I felt superior about that. The most obvious maxim is that everybody dies, and that means us, and it means our families. Grief is inevitable for *all* of us.

Grief is the emotional response to loss. Loss comes in an infinite variety of forms. Grief is not at all simple—another reason to read and learn about it. What makes it difficult is that it is a process and therefore always changing and becoming. It also varies with the type of loss. Losing a job is tough but not in the same category as losing a spouse. How we experience grief varies widely, and culture also makes a difference. As Sullender says, "How a British gentleman expresses his grief would be worlds apart from how a similar Iranian man would express his grief."[2] Yet there are commonalities based in the human condition.

Therefore, we need to learn to acknowledge grief and to own it honestly. An old Turkish proverb says, "He who conceals his grief finds no remedy for it." Grief has power. It will not be denied. It cannot be dismissed. It demands attention and will get it one way or another.

Holmes and Rahe showed a long time ago that our physical health is related to the degree of our psychological stress.[3] This has proven true in particular for people undergoing conjugal bereavement. As Scott Sullender has indicated, "There are higher rates of death, suicide, office visits to physicians and use of psychological and clergy services for the bereaved during the first year of conjugal bereavement. In the grief reaction to the

---

1. Scott Sullender reflects this difference of opinion in the following comment taken from his review of Melissa Kelley's book, *Grief: Contemporary Theory and the Practice of Ministry*: "Dr. Kelley, as the title of this book suggests, makes 'grief' into an all-encompassing process. It might be better if we return the term grief to the affect domain and find another word to describe what now appears to be such a comprehensive, multidimensional, and complex process." Sullender, "Grief's Multi-dimensional Nature," 113.

2. Sullender, *Grief and Growth*, 25.

3. Holmes and Rahe, "Rating Scale," 213–18.

sudden death of a spouse, we potentially see grief in its most dramatic and dangerous form."[4]

Even more acute is the loss of a child. Geoffrey Gorer calls this "the most distressing and long-lasting of all griefs."[5] Partly, this is due to how comparatively rare it is in modern Western societies. Above all, though, it troubles us deeply because it is so unnatural and untimely, against the natural order of things. The death of parents is at least a normal life-cycle event. In Africa, where so many children have died of AIDS and TB and other diseases treated routinely in the West, the grief experienced is incalculable.

But death is not the only loss that causes grief. Permanent loss of significant others happens all too frequently through divorce. Mel Krantzler writes that "Divorce is indeed a death, a death of a relationship; and just as the death of someone close to us brings on a period of mourning during which we come to terms with our loss, so too marital break-up is followed by a similar period of mourning."[6] All sorts of losses may accompany a divorce, each of which brings grief. This may include loss of a home, a job, a financial status, or friends. Children may lose one parent or some time with each parent—and certainly they lose the family they had known. The break-up of deep friendships, which in some ways can be more virtuous and emotionally intimate than sexual relationships, lead to profound grief also. The amount of grief in society as a whole, from all these sources, is staggering. When undiagnosed it can result in all kinds of personal and social ills.

One significant difference between the loss of a spouse through divorce and through death, highlighted by Scott Sullender, is that divorce is a more ambiguous event, meaning it can include both positive and negative emotions. When it is unwelcomed and shocking, it clearly causes grief. When it results from years of bitter conflict and attempts to repair a relationship that has proved unfruitful, feelings are more ambivalent and may include relief. However, even in this case there will be guilt, fear, and grief. Sullender's considerable experience of counseling divorced people led him to conclude that "No matter how much they say they may hate each other, there usually have been some good occasions: some happy moments, some productive years, and some positive aspects to the marriage that can be

---

4. Sullender, *Grief and Growth*, 8. Here Sullender is relying on Parkes, *Bereavement*, chapter 2.

5. Cited in Sullender, *Grief and Growth*, 8.

6. Krantzler, *Creative Divorce*, 70.

the cause for regret and sorrow. If nothing else, those married years are years spent, even years wasted, never to be relived again."[7] He adds, "I have listened to many a bitter divorcee angrily trying to persuade me, 'I could care less about that bum. He doesn't affect me anymore. I'm over him!' Such a person is not 'over it' until both the anger *and* the sorrow have been dealt with fully. Grief . . . is a function of *attachment*, not love. Strong love and strong anger are both forms of attachment."[8]

A great deal of grief is experienced by children, who often cannot process it until much later in life. I had not known bereavement until my Sharon died in 2008. I had not lost either of my parents before that. I had known grief, however. I had lost my parents, emotionally speaking, when as a boy at the tender age of six I was sent to boarding school five hundred miles away for eight months of the year. The grief of that loss lay dormant until my early thirties, when I underwent a serious clinical depression.

Married couples who have difficulty conceiving also go through pain that is all the more excruciating because it is a silent pain. They encounter it every time they meet parents with kids. But parents who are given children enter an arena where the potential for pain is greater still, with the possible loss that an untimely death may bring. And if the mother of my children dies, I grieve on their behalf as well as my own. This says nothing of all the pain of disappointments that children can bring as they grow up, through the bumps and knocks that are inevitable. You never stop parenting, I have observed. So no matter what your lot is, don't envy the other. We are all going to experience pain, and there's no use denying it, and it is not a Christian virtue to do so.

Another reason to look at death and loss is that we will die our own deaths one day. We will experience the loss and grief of that impending separation ourselves. T. S. Eliot, echoing Dante, says, "I had not thought death had undone so many."[9] We are "undone" by death in our culture. The ideals, indeed idolatries, of modern Western culture mitigate against any consideration of our own deaths. Sadly, that means we consider our own lives very little also. Not many pastors prepare their parishioners to die well by enabling them to live well, as was the case for the Puritan pastors. Richard John Neuhaus summed up our desperate lostness as a culture in this regard:

7. Sullender, *Grief and Growth*, 10.

8. Ibid.

9. Cited in Neuhaus, *Eternal Pity*, 1.

The work of dying well is, in largest part, the work of living well. Most of us are at ease in discussing what makes for a good life, but we typically become tongue-tied and nervous when discussion turns to a good death. As children of a culture radically, even religiously, devoted to youth and health, many find it incomprehensible, indeed offensive, that the word "good" should in any way be associated with death.[10]

I invite you into this journey in the belief that loss and grief can be redemptive. Redemption is possible through our losses and grieving. However, an important point to be made is that our transformation through it, and God's redemptive work in it, are *not* inevitable. We must be "exercised" or trained by it, if we are to be fruitful (Heb 12:11). It may be too early for me to speak of grief's fecundity in my own life. The seed has barely fallen into the ground and died. If there is even a green stalk, that's about it. I can only tell you how I am journeying and hope that as I share comfort with you, this may be the harvest God promises.

Knowing God and Knowing Grief

The driving motivation for writing this narrative and commentary on grief, however, relates to the ongoing task of helping others towards an understanding of grief. This involves the integration of insights on grief from Christian theology and insights from contemporary theories in the field of psychology and psychiatry. We assign a whole section to this integrative task. There is a major emphasis on the primacy of trinitarian theology, though our approach will hopefully also be integrative. Not that there haven't been some profoundly integrative and helpful accounts of grief in Christian literature.[11] That task is, however, unfinished and ongoing. For example, Scott Sullender, in his recent review of Melissa Kelley's 2010 book

---

10. Neuhaus, *Eternal Pity*, 1.

11. Some examples of a narrative approach are those of C. S. Lewis, *A Grief Observed*; Jerry Sittser, *A Grace Disguised*; Nicholas Wolterstorff, *Lament for a Son;* and Richard John Neuhaus, ed. *The Eternal Pity*. A psychologically informed Christian devotional I found helpful is the work of Raymond R. Mitsch and Lynn Brookside, *Grieving the Loss of Someone You Love*. Phil Zylla's excellent treatment of suffering, *The Roots of Sorrow*, is very much theologically integrated, but it is not primarily about bereavement grief. There are other psychologically informed accounts, like for example that in Sullender, *Grief and Growth*.

Grief,[12] states that he "could not agree more with the author . . . when she says that there has been a 'substantial disconnection between the world of ministry and the secular world of grief research, theory and care.'"[13] He adds that her "volume aims to correct that deficit by presenting readers with an overview of contemporary topics in grief research and then discussing the implications of said research for the practice of ministry." While affirming that she accomplishes the first aim, "by presenting a clear, concise, readable summary of grief studies and the work of scholars in the field . . . plus its excellent bibliography," he states with regard to "exploring the implications for ministerial practice," that "she addresses [this] all too briefly and only in suggestive ways."[14]

There are not many systematic accounts of this integration. A subject as mysterious and pain-filled as grief tends not to lend itself to analytical accounts, which is understandable. We hope here to approach the analytical aspects via personal narrative and practical information, moving toward a more formally integrative account of grief and its resolution. There will be a special emphasis on trinitarian perspectives on personhood, on comfort in grief, on adaptation to grief and growth through grief, and on psychological accounts consonant with this theology.

There is a paucity of material on grief that comes *first* from a theological and specifically *participational* perspective, and material that *also* shows awareness of the psychological literature and insights. All truth is God's truth. Theologically oriented treatments of this topic are prone to neglect the psychological insights, and this is to fail to recognize the value of insights from general revelation. Lack of psychological awareness is not a virtue.

The Christian is called to form a lived theology that is *encyclopedic*; that is, one that responds to all reality, all revelation. However, there is a priority in this revelation. The *first order* priority is confessional, historic, trinitarian theology. Pastoral theology in the past five decades has tended to be so focused on the *second order*—on theological and anthropological insights gained from the social sciences—that the gospel, and its great revelation of the being and action of the Triune God for us, has been eclipsed

12. Melissa M. Kelley is Assistant Professor of Pastoral Care and Counseling at Boston College School of Theology and Ministry. Her book's full title is *Grief: Contemporary Theory and the Practice of Ministry*.

13. Sullender, "Grief's Multi-dimensional Nature," 113–15, quote from Kelly, *Grief*, 2.

14. Sullender, "Grief's Multi-dimensional Nature," 113.

in the care and cure of souls.[15] I hope to offer a treatment of grief, its nature and role and amelioration, that is first grounded in the gospel of the Triune God of grace, who draws broken and wounded humanity into himself, and who shares the grief of every human person. I hope to approach this topic in a manner that reflects truth in every realm, including that of the human mind and affections.

What follows in this book, then, is an integrative and participational approach in which we have tried to bring the best insights of the psychology of grief into conversation with the insights of first-order Christian theology about the human person and psyche. This is, however, an asymmetric relationship. Revelation gained from the Word of God will always trump that gained by science, even though we must listen fully to science. What we are seeking is not an independent psychology, or an independent theology of psychology, but a *second-order theology of the human psyche,* one that is the result of honest and diligent research of psychology as well as what we know to be true of Scripture *as properly interpreted,* with the confidence that because all truth is God's truth, they cannot ultimately contradict. This approach is *participational,* because the study and discovery of truth from Scripture is not possible apart from our union with Christ and the guiding of the Spirit, who leads us into all truth, and because our study of the sciences as humans must be in the same way—as those fully alive in Christ to his world! The Christian who is becoming fully human again is fully alive to the Word and fully alive to the world. As Justin Roberts has said, "Christ's scandalous particularity and the attestation of the glories of God which flow through creation have been less than harmonious dancing partners" in the history of Christian thought. That is, "a theology of the cross and a theology encompassing of nature"[16] continue to require harmonization, and this is certainly true for psychological science.

In sum, we want to offer a second-order theology of the psychology of grief by bringing psychological science into conversation with an essential doctrine of the Christian faith, the first-order doctrine of the Trinity. This is the reality that God is three interpenetrated persons; persons of irreducible identity, yet persons in a mutuality of communion. God created humans in his image, to be image-bearing persons-in-relation. We will therefore look within the psychological literature for theories that postulate a consonant

15. See Andrew Purves's expose of pastoral theological trends in the introduction to his *Reconstructing Pastoral Theology.*

16. Roberts, *Behold Our God,* 5.

view of the nature of the human person as a relational or as "interpersonal self" (the interpersonal self [Bowlby], relational ontology [Fairbairn]). Understanding who God is and therefore who we are, in the spirit of Calvin's double-knowledge, is crucial to an awareness of what loss and grief are. We will especially be focused on attachment theory, which presents a particularly relational view of humanity, compatible with the biblical view of humans made in the image of the relational God. This relational view, evoking the life of attachment to God that brings needed comfort into our adaptation to grief, will provide particular insights for the journey.

Insights from relational and aesthetic theology will also reveal the Triune God as the comforting home of the soul for all who seek him, the "God of all comfort"; the Son as ultimate sympathizer, and the Spirit as comforter. Experiencing the God who has participated in our humanity and pain, and in whose life we participate now, is the heart of our grief-sharing message. He shares in our suffering; we share in his. And grief-sharing with God will also extend to grief-sharing with the people of God, bringing the power of community into the midst of loss and the resolution of grief.

Principal Motif—Grief-Sharing

This leads us to offer a primary motif for considering loss and grief and its adaptation. This is the motif of grief-sharing. This incorporates three main ideas:

i.   Grief arises because of our giving of ourselves as persons to love other persons, our sharing in the souls of those we love.

ii. Grief is shared by the God of love who, in Christ our Great High Priest, shares our suffering and is active towards us, especially in our losses, bringing sympathy and transforming grace.

iii. A component in the healing of grief is community with other human persons, though this is a sharing that must preserve both the communal nature of persons and the irreducible identity and idiosyncratic nature of the persons in community.

Before saying more about what grief is, and how it can be processed and become redemptive in our lives, I need to say a little about how I know what I am professing to know: How do we "do knowledge"? What are the limits of our knowledge? What can we know about death? What can we know about grief? And what do theology and psychology have to contribute to our knowledge? How do these disciplines of human knowledge relate? Answering those questions takes us to the next chapter.

chapter 3

The Mystery in Grief and Loss

THE UNKNOWING

"The heart has reasons. . . . *I don't know that much*, but this much I know"

IN THE SPIRIT OF Richard John Neuhaus, we wish in this book to *propose* rather than *impose*[1] some reflections and counsel on the experience of death and grief. "Mystery is attended by a fitting reticence."[2]

"I don't know that much!" is the first half of our motto. A number of aspects of the experience of death and grief can be described as "mystery." What can we know about death, given we have never died? It is easy to torment myself by wondering what that moment of transition from life to death was like for Sharon. Or was it, in fact, a process? Tammy describes how during one of Carlos's last days, he saw magnificent white angels and asked Tammy to be careful not to step on them. Was he being prepared for that transition by the presence of the angels? The hard-nosed scientist might say that these were hallucinations, the product of morphine medication. But Tammy believes otherwise. And she was with him through all the phases of the journey, pain meds included. Sharon too showed remarkable serenity throughout the stages of her passing. Was this because she sensed the presence of Christ by her side, and the loving arms of the Father? No doubt, but what role did the morphine play? Despite being drugged heavily, people still can manifest a restless spirit as they are dying. Our nurses

1. Neuhaus, *Eternal Pity*, 1.
2. Ibid.

shared that women with children tend to fight the death process, trying to stay for their kids. This would be hard to prove, but it makes sense.

And what can we know about grief? We have gained some insights through theological insights and psychological theory. But much about grief is shrouded in mystery.

For one thing, when a loved one dies, no matter how well prepared we think we are, we shut down in various ways and to different degrees. We are in shock. I had been warned about this as Sharon's time of departure became imminent. I had known she had fourth-stage cancer for twenty-one months, and she had been in palliative care for three weeks. I could understand that a sudden loss, such as through a car accident, would be a shock. I might have thought I would have been prepared for that moment. But I was shocked. You never are prepared. And seven years later, I am still thawing out.

Shock, our involuntary defense mechanism, is actually a gift. This gift to fallen humanity enables us to survive the loss of our loved ones. If we did not have such a defense mechanism (or sum total of various defense mechanisms) we would not be able to continue to function, even minimally. That was certainly my experience.

With shock comes numbness and an unintentional sense of denial. Our minds cannot grasp it. Our emotions are too powerful to be processed at that time. If we did not have defense mechanisms in place, we would not be able to handle the reality of our losses. Their full impact would kill us. Samuel Clemens in his *Autobiography of Mark Twain* puts it well:

> It is one of the mysteries of our nature that a man, all unprepared, can receive a thunderstroke like that and live. There is but one reasonable explanation of it. The intellect is stunned by the shock and by groping gathers the meaning of the words. The power to realize their full import is mercifully wanting. The mind has a dumb sense of vast loss—that is all. It will take mind and memory months and possibly years to gather the details and thus learn and know the whole extent of the loss.

Why is death such a shock? On a merely naturalistic basis, as a necessary part of the human life cycle, shouldn't it be experienced as normal? In this chapter I will explore some answers to these questions. And while death is a shock, I think *grief is the process of shock thawing out*. This isn't the only dynamic at work in grief. *Why* death brings a shock reaction needs to be explained in theologically and psychologically sound ways. We will consider some of them in this chapter and others, in more detail, in the next (particularly that we are interpersonal persons). In this chapter, I want to focus on shock as a way of expressing the unknowing dynamics of death and grief.

The Mystery of Shock: The Particularity of Persons

Death is a mysterious phenomenon in many ways. Somehow we get used to its presence. Every day across the world, approximately 150,000 people die. That's approximately 6,000 every hour, but it hardly affects us. Yet when someone we know dies, it's like someone hitting us in the gut. Joseph Stalin, with the irony that a mass murderer brings to the discussion, wrote that "One death is a tragedy; a million deaths is a statistic."[3]

As Richard John Neuhaus says, "Death is the most everyday of everyday things." It's not just that thousands die every day, but that "death is the warp and woof of existence in the ordinary, the quotidian, the way things are." But, he continues, this "generality of everyday existence with which the wise have learned to live . . . is shattered, not by a sudden awareness of the generality but by the singularity of *a* death—by the death of someone we love with a love inseparable from life. . . . [I]t is death in the singular that shatters all we thought we knew about death. It is death in the singular that turns the problem of death into the catastrophe of death."[4]

There is a particularity about grief, a "thisness," which is related to the mystery of the particularity and relationality of human personhood. Neuhaus again writes, "Encountered by the singularity of the death of a particular person who had never been here before and will never be here again, we may cry out in our immeasurable sense of loss that precisely *this* catastrophe has never happened before."[5] Neuhaus also cites Arthur Schopenhauer, who emphasized the same point: "The deep pain that is felt at the death of every friendly soul arises from the feeling that there is in every individual something which is inexpressible, peculiar to him alone, and is therefore, absolutely and irretrievably lost."

3. Ibid., 2.

4. Ibid., 2.

5. Ibid., 4.

All who lose loved ones share something profound. As I discovered when my wife became a cancer sufferer, a deep, implicit sense of community binds cancer sufferers, their caregivers, and those who experience the death of spouses or children or parents. This combination of undeniable particularity about the person we have lost, and the commonality we share with others, gives us permission to be who we are in the midst of grief. It validates the particularities of how we grieve. Even in the brief description John gives us of Mary and Martha's reactions to the death of their brother Lazarus in John 11, he reflects great insight about this particularity. Martha, the active one, stays busy and expresses her anger directly at Jesus. Mary, the contemplative sister, retreats into her house and doesn't come to greet Jesus until he actually calls her: "Then Martha, as soon as she heard that Jesus was coming, went and met him, *but Mary sat still in the house.*"

So, the stock phrase that we sometimes use if we too have lost a loved one, "I know what you are going through," is only partially true and easily misunderstood. Our intent is not to rob someone of the particularity of the loved one who was lost, or to diminish the particularity of that person's grief. Nonetheless, that is often how it is heard. It is actually better to err in the other direction and say "I have no idea what you are going through," even if you have experienced your own deep loss.

The wonder of the God of the Bible is that God loves everybody personally, watches over each particular journey, and draws each one into the Big Story without any loss of identity. At death we are not assimilated into God or his creation, the universe, or absorbed into nothingness. Knowing that we retain our individuality is key for authentic grieving and moving on into growth. As useful as it may be to know that our experience is not entirely unique and in some ways matches the patterns of others, it is important to know that there are aspects that are indeed unique.

Our experience of grief is idiosyncratic. *We* need to feel *our* grief in *our* way. And we need to know that in the midst of our journey, we can affirm (as do millions of others) that "the LORD is *my* Shepherd" (Ps 23:1). He walks with us in the journey from the diagnosis or the accident or the heart attack, all the way through the watchful hours, to the point of departure, and on into the grief journey. We can enter into the personal I-Thou relationship depicted by the first verse of Psalm 16, a psalm about a person facing death: "Keep *me* safe, *my* God, for in *you I* take refuge."

The Mystery of Shock: The Interpersonal Nature of Persons

Why should grief be so deep and mysterious, so much so that one good cry doesn't resolve it? Why does it usually take at least a year to recover when a spouse dies, and why does it actually remain a wound forever? If the particularity of the person we have lost helps to explain this in part, the interpenetrated nature of the human self further explains it. Human beings, though irreducibly unique, are also profoundly mutual, profoundly interrelated, profoundly embedded in other persons. Each of us is an interpersonal self. The theological underpinnings of this will be expanded upon in chapters 5 and 6. To varying degrees, the people in our lives are part of us. Parents have a significant part in forming their children. This is true genetically and even emotionally within the womb, and from the moment of birth. When we lose a parent, we have lost something of ourselves.

Children are a part of parents too. Once I was watching my nine-year-old son play soccer. I was standing close to another father. His son had the ball, and as the man's son took a shot at goal, the father took a shot with him and kicked me right in the shin! Identification can take on unhealthy dimensions, when fathers or mothers live out their sporting careers vicariously through their children. In such co-dependence, the particularity of individuals is neglected and the identity of persons is blurred. However, even when the parent and child have a healthy interdependent relationship, the sense of community runs too deep to fathom. This is mystery. So if a child dies, we lose a deep piece of ourselves.

In marriage too, no matter whether or not the marriage is happy, two people become one in every way possible. Cognitively, emotionally, sexually. Each couple is a sacrament or sign of the Triune Godhead, in which three persons of irreducible identity are yet one in communion and essence because they are mutually internal to one another, completely interpenetrated, and completely inter-animated. Imperfect and incomplete though the echo is, the extensive intertwining of marriage partners' personalities, thought-sharing, emotional inter-dependence, and sexual intimacy actually echoes that divine interpenetration. This is part of what causes a partner's death to be so shocking.

I honestly lost a piece of my self, and not because I was unhealthily co-dependent. Marriage is about two becoming one. The sexual oneness is actually an embodied act of interpenetration that symbolizes everything else about our oneness. Death is a disruption of that. That's why it's so tough. Our psyches form a bond, and it is severed by death, and that hurts and confuses and disorients.

The Mystery of Shock: Death Is Not Natural

Another reason why death is a shock, and why grief is a shock-thawing process, is that death for human beings made in the image of God is *not* natural. Death is more than we can take in because God didn't make us to die. When God endowed human beings with his image, one aspect of that new human existence was the endowment of everlasting life.

The image of God is variously described in the history of Christian scholarship as *relationality* with God and neighbor, as *structural* (the capacity for reason and self-reflection), and as *functional* (the ability to continue God's work in the world through reproduction and work). Vital to all three, however, was the possession of spiritual life. With the endowment came the promise of its removal if sin was committed.

In the Genesis story, God told Adam and Eve that they "*must not eat from the tree of the knowledge of good and evil, for when you eat from it you will certainly die*" (2:17). One must assume that if they did not sin, they would not die. When the primal pair did sin, death came to them and to all their offspring. This was not expressed merely in the fact that they no longer lived forever, but that they were banished from the immediate presence of God that sustained their life.

Human death, even when compared to the death of animals, is unique and troublesome. The writer of Hebrews indicates that Satan "holds the power of death" (Heb 2:14), that is until that power is broken by Christ's death. Paul describes death in 1 Corinthians 15 as an "enemy," albeit an enemy that will be finally destroyed when Christ returns. In the meantime, human death is not a natural phenomenon but a specter of demonic power, a reminder of the fallenness of creation and human beings, a symbol of a primal separation between humanity and God. Later, we will look at how Christ has broken the power of death and made death for Christians a passing into his presence, which is better than current life "by far" (Phil 1:23). But for now death is an enemy still to be destroyed, a grief-evoking phenomenon even with this ultimate hope.

Death hurts. Paul expressed this realism in 1 Thessalonians 4:13, when he said, "*you do not grieve like the rest of mankind, who have no hope.*" The tacit assumption is that we *do* grieve nevertheless. This is not just because we are parted from our loved ones until the time of the resurrection, or until we go to heaven. That grief is painful, even though we will see them again. In light of the fact that humans are made in the image of God, for eternal life, they are still able to imagine this, and so death is a shock. *God is, after all, life!*

The Mystery of Shock: The Timing Is Not under Our Control

Another contributor to the shock nature of death and grief is that the exact moment of death is mysterious, and therefore always unexpected, even if it is generally expected. During Sharon's time in palliative care, I was told on two or three occasions on the basis of the best medical knowledge that Sharon's death was imminent and that it could be just hours away. I have nothing but praise and thankfulness for the medical and nursing care Sharon received at the Vancouver General Hospital, the Vancouver Cancer Agency, and the Peace Arch Palliative Care Unit. Yet each time they predicted her dying, they were incorrect. They did not predict her death on the night she actually did die. I don't have even a modicum of blame for the physicians or nurses, who tried their best to predict for our benefit. It's just not an exact science. Why not? I think God reserves the right to determine the moment of death. He watches over the death of every human being and cares specially for his covenant people.

The words *"Precious in the sight of the Lord is the death of his saints"* signal a watching-over of the death of the people of God. In fact, Paul's words in Acts 17:25 indicate that this is true for all people, whether Christian or not: *"he himself gives all people life and breath and everything else."* Many of the Psalms speak metaphorically of humans as "only a breath," and Psalm 104:29 specifically speaks of the fact that God removes that breath in his own time: "When you hide your face, they are terrified; when you take away their breath, they die and return to the dust."

Actually, you will understand if you have been through this, but as a family, we reached a time in Sharon's suffering when we were ready to let her go. She had suffered so much, and we just wanted her suffering to be over. And yet she lived on for what seemed like an eternity. I can remember at one point actually being angry with God as I sat alone by her bedside and cried out, "There's no rhyme nor reason to this! What's the point of this? Please take her, God! You won't heal her and you won't take her. What's this about?" And God spoke back quite distinctly in my heart: "She took care of you for how long, and you can't even take care of her this long? It is a privilege to care for her even when she's unconscious and unresponsive like this."

Perhaps that's a little unveiling of mystery that may help us understand why people are permitted to have years of dementia and what seems like purposeless existence, and why it is that we are not permitted to choose to end life at the volition of the patient or of any other human. All humans have a dignity that derives from their being made in the image of God. It is a privilege to care for them on God's behalf. But still there remains a mystery, in which we live by faith and seek understanding, little by little.

The Mystery of Shock: Predicting the Tears

A further aspect of the mystery of grief is the expression of emotion as we thaw out from the shock, its frequency and its intensity. Within the grief journey, we are more emotionally labile than is normal for us. We cry at unexpected times, often in embarrassing situations—if not for us, then for the people we are with. C. S. Lewis's book *A Grief Observed*, written after the loss of his wife (as depicted in the movie *Shadowlands*), was profoundly helpful to me during this period. He thought all grieving people should be locked up for a year, because it's awkward for grievers who could break down at any time and awkward for those encountering them. Even five years after Sharon left, I wasn't quite sure that folks in my classes or sermons were "safe" from my outbursts. They let me out anyway!

Of course, one should expect that people should learn to be comfortable with tears. Tears are to be treasured, for God even keeps them in a bottle (Ps. 55:8, KJV). Jesus wept on more than one occasion, and he defines both humanity in general and humanity in particular. The truth is that some cultures are more comfortable with tears than others. The important thing to say is this: *when the tears come, let them come*. They bring healing. No good can come of suppressing this emotion. You can only deny weeping for so long. It will come out one way or another. But the timing is a mystery.

During Sharon's time in palliative care, I cried a few tears, mostly when I saw my children watching her suffer or hugging her. A great deal of my weeping has been done when I think of my children having lost the most emotionally supportive and fun-loving mother a child could have. My feelings are projections of what I imagine they must feel. These feelings probably stem from my own deep sense of loss when I went to boarding school at age six and to all intents and purposes "lost" my parents.

In that time of watching Sharon deteriorate, however, I was not very present to my own emotions. I felt the need to stay strong for my kids, and to make sure that all who visited with her felt appropriately honored. Being the pastor of a large community and living in that community for eleven years meant that many people did want to visit, and this was a gift. Yet I was keenly alive to the tensions felt by visitors, who were sometimes turned away—and also to certain extended family dynamics that arose from different expectations in that regard and others.

Two days before Sharon died, I wept loudly as I went home, sensing her time was near. But it was a stifled weeping, one in which I struggled to come to grips with the unreal reality that she would really be gone. And shock was setting in. Weeping did come as I stood over her when she had died. That night when close friends brought food over, I broke down and wept sore. The first night, when I slept for the first time with the awareness that I was as a widower, lives on in my memory for its stark loneliness. Then came the busyness of setting up the memorial, so feelings again went on hold. The following days of acute grief were days in which the shock was profound—and the thawing profuse, when it came. One of the myths I have unveiled is that you ever get over this. It may become less acute, but you never do. It marks you for life. The only question is *how* it marks you.

The Mystery of Shock: From Gift to Liability

Shock and defense mechanisms are no doubt a gift of grace to humanity. Mitsch and Brookside speak of shock as "God's Anesthesia."[6] We cannot possibly process the full reality that the death of a loved one represents. Our full sensibility, closed down at first, slowly and sporadically opens up as we can face the reality of our loss. However, the shock we experience as gift in the initial stages can, after a while, be detrimental to facing the realities of our loss and our feelings. This inertia can complicate the grief process and delay feeling all the emotions that loss entails. When grief counselors speak of working *through* and not *around* grief, this implies some struggle. Many people have a tendency to avoid emotions. It takes work to become present to our emotions and to seek their resolution. The passivity of the numbness phase does at some point need to move on to activity, to a phase of doing

6. Mitsch and Brookside, *Grieving the Loss*, 40.

the work of grief resolution. In a later chapter we will look at this in more detail. Suffice it to say that working through grief is worth it.

One of the most important convictions that undergirds this book is the great mystery that loss and grief can, in the divine economy, become redemptive. Redemption is possible through these losses, but that transformation is not inevitable. It requires us to be "exercised" or trained by it, as per the writer of the Hebrews. In chapter 12, having just told his readers (v. 10) that they can actually participate in the holiness of God through God's loving discipline in our lives, he re-emphasizes in verse 11 the need for our action in this participational relationship with God, by which he imparts his holiness to us: *"No discipline seems pleasant at the time, but painful. Later on, however, it produces a harvest of righteousness and peace for those who have been trained by it"* (12:11). Clearly, active work is necessary.

The time for mentioning this to bereaved people is *not* immediately after their loss, nor even when they are in the shock-dominated acute phase of grief. Purely supportive presence and counsel is appropriate then. There will come a time, however, when we can sensitively help people begin to come to terms with comforting theological realities, and when we can encourage them in the work of grief resolution, and with an openness to what God wants to do *in* them through their tragic loss. God is not the author of evil. He does permit it, and he redeems it in ways that somehow transcend what may have transpired had there been no evil. Each chapter from this point on will speak about an aspect of the gracious redemptiveness of grief.

The author of Hebrews speaks of two phases in the experience of painful events: *at the time* and *later on*. To reiterate, the character growth that is spoken of *later on* is conditional upon our being *trained by it*. That fecundity is dependent upon a certain exercise of the soul. This involves a posture towards God, a teachability, a softness of heart. It also involves practices that give space for God to work. He works in us as we work out our salvation. His work and ours are compatible, not contradictory. The emphasis is on his work, so this is an asymmetric compatibility. But our grief work is nevertheless an essential component of our growth. "We can either get better or get bitter" is the popular saying, and it is true.

Complications can accompany grief, especially if the inertia towards feeling our feelings is not overcome. These complications can include unresolved anger, manifesting in distant relationships or relationships damaged by uncontrolled rage, anxiety, or depression. Having suffered from depression since my early thirties, I was afraid that losing Sharon might plunge me into a deep depression. On the contrary, I believe that the counseling I had undergone over the years for depression actually prepared me somewhat for experiencing and processing the emotions associated with grief.

Feeling sadness and experiencing anger in a healthy way were two areas of emotional life in which I was greatly broken growing up, for a number of reasons—some cultural or genetic (Scottish reserve), and some circumstantial. I had not processed my loss when I went to a missionary boarding school five hundred miles from my parents. There is some evidence for a link between losses in childhood and the occurrence of depression in adulthood.[7]

For a child who was effectively orphaned, the loss itself was significant. But in that era and setting, there was little emotional awareness, openness, or support. Additionally, this setting was characterized by emotional suppression. Well-meaning people believed that making this kind of sacrifice was part of the life of dedication to the work of the Lord.

I do not hold a grudge against my parents for what they did, for I believe they were sincere and that they did valuable missional work. I do, however, maintain the viewpoint that they and many others in the missionary movement of the last century failed to weigh the importance of the creation orders of Genesis, which includes the valuing of marriage and family. There was a deficit in this missionary era of creational and image-bearing theology, as well as in psychological awareness with respect to the development of children. Missionaries did not seem to see the Great Commission within the context of the cultural mandate. Jesus' teachings about the primacy of obedience to the call of God over family do relativize family,[8] and they do call us away from any idolatry of family. But they should not be interpreted as contradicting the value of children, who are to be nourished and cherished. The call of the gospel restores humanity; it does not deny it. Sending children to boarding school is not a humanly nourishing act.

The effects of this experience on my emotional development, and that of many others in this situation, have been significant. I carried a residue of anger and pain under the surface until my early thirties. I was driven in many areas and was unable to relate intimately with my wife and kids. In

---

7. See Janice L. Krupnick, "Bereavement during Childhood and Adolescence," ch. 5 in Osterweis, Solomon, and Green, eds., *Bereavement: Reactions, Consequences, and Care.*

8. This is reflected in Teresa of Avila, in the title of a chapter in *The Way of Perfection*: "Oh how good it is for those who have left the world to flee from relatives and how they find truer friends." Teresa, *Way of Perfection*, 115.

my early thirties, Sharon was so exasperated with my emotional disconnectedness and workaholic drive that she could no longer express her love for me. Her withdrawal triggered in me a massive sense of loss that went back to those boarding school days. This plunged me into a deep, suicidal depression with some psychosis.

I went through several years of intensive therapy with an excellent psychiatrist who, with insight arising from psychodynamic therapeutic training and spiritual discernment, gave me incalculable gifts. Not only because I wept cathartically for the first time as an adult, and not only because I uncovered a load of pain and anger that had fueled my inordinate drive for academic success and fame, along with much vocational ambivalence, but because it enabled me to begin to break free from aloofness and become more engaged in relationships. I received the ability to discover a God-given aspect of my being: my heart, my affections, my emotions, both positive and negative. The challenge of getting me to *experience* my anger was considerable. I had built up many skillful ways of avoiding and redirecting anger into workaholism and dogged competitiveness on the sports field. Discovering that feelings were embodied—that I could sense them in my body, and learn to press into them, listen to and process them, without necessarily acting on them—was a gift.

I wept a lot in those sessions. I slew some giants. I was welcomed into humanity by the psychiatrist. That is, I was brought into solidarity with every other human on God's earth who is broken. I discovered I had been wearing an "S" on my shirt for "Superman," a superman who could not feel and could not enter into his own brokenness, and who found ways to stay aloof from his own feelings and most other people's too. After a while, I became much more emotionally available to Sharon. She responded with grace. After that period, she would always say when asked by elders or search committees about our marriage, that it was "ten out of ten." I became much more comfortable dealing with crises in the lives of parishioners. Having encountered my own insecurities, I became able to enter in to the pain and insecurities of the people in the church I served. I began also to experience God in ways that transformed my worship, and that showed in sermons much more attuned to the heart of humanity. I became much more in tune with God, able to express worship with my whole being, not just my intellect. This was such a gift.

The grief-sharing character of God was particularly real to me as I found healing from the acute phase of my depression. One incident will suffice to express this. During the depression, Sharon became ill with hepatitis A, contracted in an unsanitary restaurant. Life during the season when she was bedridden, looking after two young children and continuing to serve as a pastor, was challenging to say the least. One particularly preachers'-blue Monday, I had had no time for my usual lengthy Scripture readings, and I had worked all day to get the kids to school, do the housework and meal preparation, keep the wretched floors free of pesky crumbs, etc., etc., . . . the anger in me was mounting. Late at night, after getting the kids to bed, I still had to buy groceries. Off I drove to the local supermarket. Traffic lights that failed to turn fast enough received torrents of rage. I got to the supermarket, found what I needed, cursed the teller under my breath for her slowness, packed the groceries in my car and headed off home. I looked across at the passenger seat and saw a cassette tape with music on it by Richard Allen Farmer, whose worship leading I had encountered at a pastors' conference. My first thought was, "That's the last thing I want to do right now—listen to Christian music!" Something, someone, made me place it in the tape deck nevertheless. The song that played was an old hymn I knew from my youth, which he had dressed up a little. The words were these:

> Loved with everlasting love, led by grace that love to know,
> Spirit breathing from above, Thou hast taught me it is so,
> Oh what full and perfect peace, Oh what rapture all divine,
> In a love which cannot cease, I am His and He is mine.
> In a love which cannot cease, I am His and He is mine.

I began to feel, in a way, more real than ever before, a sense of the immediate love and gentle embrace of the Father. I began to weep. There was something personal about God's grief-sharing with me that night. The third and fourth verses seemed to remind me that God had been with me all those years, back when I was at boarding school. That he had watched over all my days and was nestling me in his providential arms. That he was shaping me in it all. And that he would never leave me.

> Things that once were wild alarms cannot now disturb my rest;
> Closed in everlasting arms, pillowed on the loving breast
> Oh to lie forever here, doubt and care and self resign;
> Whilst he whispers in my ear, I am his and he is mine.
> Whilst he whispers in my ear, I am his and he is mine.

His forever, Only His, who the Lord and me shall part?

Ah, with what a rest of bliss Christ can fill the loving heart!

Heav'n and earth may fade and flee, firstborn light in gloom decline;

But while God and I shall be, I am his and he is mine.

But while God and I shall be, I am his and he is mine.[9]

It is hard to convey how these words became more than words, but an entrance to a divine encounter that night. When I got home, Sharon could see that something had happened. She saw the evidence of tears—I had wept for probably ten minutes of sore crying that was God-filled, peace-filled, joyful.

When I recounted this story to the psychiatrist, her comment was, "Yes, Ross, and did you notice, you received this gracious revelation from God on the day you least deserved it?" At least to my way of thinking, I had least deserved it. I had not read the Scriptures, I had not prayed, I had been irritable most of the day. This is the real God, the God who shares in our grief by sometimes giving us massive outpourings of his love when we least deserve it. He doesn't ever love us because we deserve it. He just loves us.

I have often said, when recounting my journey with depression, that having depression morphed me from teacher into pastor-teacher. Judith McBride, the psychiatrist I am speaking of, said many memorable things. In the midst of a session in which I manifested a lot of the self-hatred and guilt that characterizes *melancholia*, I commented that I had just received an invitation to consider the senior pastorate of a church much larger than the one I was serving (large, by Canadian standards). "But what right have I to be a pastor in any church? Look at me! Depressed. Who wants a depressed pastor?" She responded in the serene and deeply penetrative way that so characterized her counseling, "Ross, your greatest brokenness will be your greatest ministry." Those words continue to be true. This is the redemptive nature of grief.

An infinite number of losses can trigger grief in humans. Break-ups between dating teenagers evoke grief that is complicated by a sense of rejection. Where do these broken hearts go? Parents of teenagers may easily dismiss such feelings, but they can be painful experiences of abandonment and lost self-esteem. Kids who are left out of the inner circle at school, or who are bullied, also grieve what they imagine normality might be. When pastors leave congregations, there can be a profound sense of loss for both

9. George Wade Robinson (1838–77).

pastor and congregation. With this often comes a sense of idealization of the former pastor that makes things difficult for the incoming one. Church members tell each other he just can't preach like his predecessor. And most important, Pastor So and So "never did it that way." Such idealization is a symptom of grief, and congregations need to grieve the loss of a long-term pastor before inviting a new pastor to come. Pastors who have formed deep bonds over a number of years with a congregation also need a grieving period.

Pain is a reality in this period of the world's redemptive history. Single people who want desperately to be married have pain. They imagine that somehow being married would mean a loss of suffering. Yet people who take the risk of marrying are actually stepping into an arena in which the pain of eventual loss is almost inevitable. And as C. S. Lewis said it, "Bereavement is a universal and integral part of the experience of love."[10] Or as Hilary Stanton Zunin has written, "The risk of love is loss, and the price of loss is grief. But the pain of grief is only a shadow when compared with the pain of never risking love."[11]

So when I experienced the loss of the closest friend and lover of my life, I was somewhat prepared by this emotional training. Not that I didn't undergo shock, and cry many tears, and still fight the tendencies to avoidance, but I was able to get through without plunging into a fresh episode of depression. Many men in Western culture do not have the emotional awareness necessary to deal with their emotions. When grief strikes, they are at a loss. It is important for simply being "fully human" to discover our hearts, to know our affections, to discern our emotions, so that we can truly love God with heart, mind, and strength, and our neighbor as ourselves.

Having acknowledged much mystery in the area of death and loss and grief, we now consider some things we can know . . . .

---

10. Lewis, *A Grief Observed*, 41.

11. Cited in full in Brandon, *Treasures*, 154–55. See also Zunin and Zunin, *Art of Condolence*, 11.

chapter 4

How We Know What We Do Know

"The heart has reasons . . . I don't know that much, but *this much I know.*"

AN INCREASING NUMBER OF people are writing books about a near- or beyond-death experience, and some of their reports of having seen Jesus and heaven sound plausible. But these experiences can never be taken as hard proof of what the Bible conveys—for various reasons, including the fact that the human brain is capable of remarkable powers. It may be evidence, but not proof. Modern philosophy, in contrast with those who believe their experience has unveiled all the mystery, acknowledges that death is beyond our human experience and therefore encourages complete agnosticism concerning death. Not much is even said by modern philosophy about death, as it is—as Neuhaus observes—"an irrational event, that inconveniently disrupts a world that's otherwise under rational control. It is a subject pushed to the side, best left to the specialists of medical and therapeutic technique."[1] The trouble with this approach, as Neuhaus indicates, is that "The result is a weirdly unreal view of reality, a kingdom of let's-pretend-things-are-not-as-they-are." Then he cites the poem of Edna St. Vincent Millay:

> Childhood is not from birth to a certain age and at a certain age.
> The child is grown, and puts away childish things.
> Childhood is the kingdom where nobody dies.

1. Neuhaus, *Eternal Pity*, 5.

Nobody that matters, that is.[2]

Philosophy, specifically of the Anglo-American analytic school, suggests that nothing meaningful can be said about death. "Those who are alive do not *know* death in a way that makes it subject to rational analysis."[3] But this has not always been the way of doing philosophy. The ancients said that "all philosophy begins in wonder." "With some exceptions," says Neuhaus, "contemporary philosophy stops at wonder." We are told not to wonder about what we can't know for sure. This is passing strange, for as Neuhaus indicates,

> the most important things of everyday life we cannot know for sure. We cannot *know* them beyond all possibility of their turning out to be false. We order our loves and loyalties, we invest our years with meaning and our death with hope, not knowing for sure, beyond all reasonable doubt, whether we might not have gotten it wrong. What we need is a philosophy that enables us to speak truly, if not clearly, a wisdom that does not eliminate but comprehends our doubt.[4]

The way we know what we know (epistemology) is not simply by using the faculty of reason. Though reason is a crucial piece in knowing, and a God-given gift to image-bearing humans, the idea that we can use pure reason to know everything we know is actually pure myth. Science did not develop under the ancient Greek philosophers precisely because they had no use for empirical discovery. They believed they could understand or idealize their way to knowledge. The idea that experiments might be helpful did not occur to them because matter was a lesser reality than spirit and intellect. They were great mathematicians but not great scientists. From the Enlightenment and onward, empiricism and reason together came to be considered as the way to know. Anything science could not discover in this way was considered as *values*, but not true *knowledge* that could be shared in the public square. Faith and reason were incompatible. All mystery would be resolved by science, given enough time. Tacit ways of knowing were discounted. In modernity, science has become the ultimate arbiter of truth in the public realm. Faith and values, which can't be proven or quantified, have been assigned to the less authoritative private sphere.

2. Ibid.
3. Ibid.
4. Ibid.

As products of the Western Enlightenment or modernity, we tend to come at knowledge, or how we know what we know, in this direction: we use reason, and when we have reached the limits of reason, we may exercise faith. When even faith doesn't reveal what we can know, then we reluctantly acknowledge mystery.

The better insights of postmodernity have exposed the myth of pure reason, the ideal that reason can ever be unbiased. Philosophers like Michael Polanyi have also exposed the myth that science is free from prejudice. When science isolates questions that are tested by experiment, it can provide accurate answers based on reason. However, the *philosophy* of science, which seeks answers to the broader questions of the cosmos, is subject to the same interpretive issues as other realms of knowledge. Postmodernity has thus debunked modernity's myth that pure, unprejudiced reason exists, exposing the fact that all suppositions have presuppositions while acknowledging ways of knowing that are tacit.

The Christian way of knowing has always acknowledged that faith is a crucial part of knowing. In the Christian tradition we encounter mystery, and with a faith posture, we seek understanding. Faith is always intertwined with reason, and both are exercised in response to mystery. On this account, faith is *a way of knowing*, not a leap in the dark. Christianity is a reasonable faith. This is the "faith seeking understanding" approach of the Christian tradition since Augustine and Anselm. This approach is, I think, consonant with that of *critical realism*, a term used in general philosophy.

> In the philosophy of perception, critical realism is the theory that some of our sense-data (for example, those of primary qualities) can and do accurately represent external objects, properties, and events, while other of our sense-data (for example, those of secondary qualities and perceptual illusions) do not accurately represent any external objects, properties, and events. Put simply, critical realism highlights a mind-dependent aspect of the world that reaches to understand (and comes to understanding of) the mind-independent world.[5]

Critical realism has, under the influence of Roy Bhaskar, been used particularly of the philosophy of perception in the social sciences. It has also been applied specifically to describe the approach of a significant number of scientist-theologians (T. F. Torrance, John Polkinghorne, Ian Barbour, Arthur Peacocke, Alister McGrath, and Wentzel van Huyssteen) in

---

5. http://en.wikipedia.org/wiki/Critical_realism_(philosophy_of_perception).

the school of Bernard Lonergan and Michael Polanyi. These scholars have sought to demonstrate that the languages of science and of Christian theology, and the way to knowledge in each, is similar, forming a starting point for a dialogue between them. N. T. Wright, New Testament scholar and retired Bishop of Durham (Anglican), has also expressed his belief in this way of knowing: "I propose a form of critical realism. This is a way of describing the process of 'knowing' that acknowledges the reality of the thing known, as something other than the knower (hence 'realism'), while fully acknowledging that the only access we have to this reality lies along the spiralling path of appropriate dialogue or conversation between the knower and the thing known (hence 'critical')."[6] Biblical and scientist-theologians share the notion that absolute certainty is an unreachable goal this side of heaven, but we may be reasonably confident about knowledge when the evidence is weighed carefully, and when it is self-consistent.

When it comes to the theology and psychology of grief, I will follow this approach. Encountering the mystery with wonder, seeking insight with faith and understanding together, and taking refuge in the solidities of what we can know by revelation will hopefully lead to an approach to caring for the grieving that is not reductionistic or simplistic, but realistic (critically and affectively) and respectful of the idiosyncratic nature of grief as well as its commonalities. This critically realistic approach to what we know personally and theologically will be reflected in a phrase that recurs throughout the book: "Mystery and certainties in loss: I don't know that much, but this much I know."

This, then, is a way of knowing that includes rather than neglects faith. Knowing begins with encountering mystery and revelation with wonder and then pursuing understanding in faith. So something can be said about grief, death, and resurrection. To be sure, the Christian way of knowing about things, including death and grief, must remain a humble way, because it involves both mystery and faith. Dogmatism beyond what has been revealed is not a truly Christian way of knowing.

Does that mean Christians cannot know anything? God has revealed himself in human history through his Son Jesus Christ, who entered history, became one with humanity, entered into death and rose again vicariously for us.[7] Through the Old Testament Scriptures that anticipated him,

---

6. Wright, *New Testament and the People of God*, 35.

7. "There exists no document from the ancient world, witnessed by so excellent a set of textual and historical testimonies and offering so superb an array of historical data on

and the New Testament that then interpreted him, God has spoken about who he is, and about salvation for humanity, and about things like death and resurrection. The church has received this, and a rich intellectual tradition has arisen in response. The revelation is self-consistent, and it has been found to be true by millions of believers. This is a critically realistic approach to what we know personally and theologically. We will seek refuge in the certainties of what we can know about death and resurrection and loss and grief, by revelation—and at the same time, we will allow for the mystery of death and grief, admitting that there are limits to what we can know, and press into the mystery with humility and wonder.

As I encounter the mystery of death and loss and grief, by faith in God's revelation in his Son Jesus and the written Word of God, I have come to know that death has had its sting removed by Jesus' death and resurrection. He is present by the Spirit to comfort us in the present and to give us hope for the future. By revelation I have come to the understanding that human persons are reflectors of the Triune God, and that they are therefore profoundly relational persons, intertwined in the other, and that there are profound depths to their inner being. By revelation I have come to know also that sin has entered the world, bringing not just the obvious calamities of disease and death, but the more subtle disorientations and pathologies and brokennesses that result from disconnectedness from God and each other. *This much I know.* I have not forsaken my reason to believe any of that, but ultimately I know I have taken a step of faith. Faith is reasonable, in

---

which an intelligent decision may be made. An honest person cannot dismiss a source of this kind. Skepticism regarding the historical credentials of Christianity is based upon an irrational bias." Pinnock, *Set Forth Your Case,* 58. "Some writers may toy with the fancy of a 'Christ-myth,' but they do not do so on the ground of historical evidence. The historicity of Christ is as axiomatic for an unbiased historian as the historicity of Julius Caesar. It is not historians who propagate the 'Christ-myth' theories." Bruce, *New Testament Documents,* 123. Professor Thomas Arnold, for fourteen years a headmaster of Rugby, author of the famous *History of Rome* and appointed to the chair of modern history at Oxford, was well acquainted with the value of evidence in determining historical facts. He said: "I have been used for many years to study the histories of other times, and to examine and weigh the evidence of those who have written about them, and I know of no one fact in the history of mankind which is proved by better and fuller evidence of every sort, to the understanding of a fair inquirer, than the great sign which God hath given us that Christ died and rose again from the dead." Cited in Smith, *Therefore Stand,* 425–26. Note, these evidences are historical and legal, not scientific. One cannot do a test to see if the resurrection of Jesus is reproducible. At the end of time the resurrection of humanity will be the acid test. Until then, we have good historical evidence, but not scientific proof. Faith would not be necessary if we did have proof.

light of the revelation of God in history, in the person of his Son who lived and died and rose again in real history. However, the mystery of death as we experience it in this era where the kingdom has already come and yet has not fully come, is still very much just that—a mystery. There's a lot *we just don't know*. A lot about the deep human psyche. A lot about exactly how the loss of the other affects us. A lot about how our shock response protects us. A lot about the idiosyncratic nature of individual persons and how they grieve and recover. A lot about exactly how our own sin's self-orientation warps our personalities, and a lot about how our relational patterns are affected when we are sinned against. A lot about what will bring comfort to one particular bereaved person and not another. A lot I just don't know about what exactly the future resurrection life looks like.

Sources of Knowledge

The sources of knowledge for Christians can be broken down into three main types of revelation. First is God's *personal* revelation. God has revealed himself and continues to reveal himself personally; that is, in and through the person of his Son, Jesus Christ our Lord, and through the person of the Holy Spirit, who awakens our spiritual senses to receive revelation so as to be regenerated by it. This personal revelation has been made to us primarily through the written Word of God, the Scriptures, written by many human authors but supervised by the work of the Holy Spirit, so that what these human authors wrote is what God wanted to write. This is called *special* revelation. The writing styles and grammatical nuances of the human authors were preserved in a manner that was compatible with what God wanted to say, and with how he wanted to say it.

The church encountered, received, and interpreted this revelation, and in time, crafted some essentialist creeds that summarize the Christian faith. The Niceno-Constantinopolitan Creed is one that the ancient church affirmed, both in its Eastern (what became the Eastern Orthodox Church, centered in Constantinople, now Istanbul) and Western (what became the Roman Catholic Church) communities. The basic affirmation of the Christian faith as expressed by the creeds is now upheld by the Orthodox, Catholic, and Protestant traditions. This is what might be termed *first-order* theology. What we think about death and resurrection, about the nature of the human psyche, about loss and grieving, is first and foremost a reflection on God's personal and special revelation, and is bounded by it.

Revelation is a communion category. In other words, God reveals himself to people who are in communion or fellowship with him. Before there can be communion, there has to be union. Thus, revelation is received when we have been brought into union with Christ by the Spirit's regenerating work, which first awakens us from spiritual death; it is received by the Spirit's illuminating work, which opens our spiritual eyes to see the beauty of Christ and understand spiritual truth; and it is received by the Spirit's indwelling, which bonds us to Christ. As people intertwined in Christ and therefore as his church, as people loved by and loving him, as people empowered by his Spirit—this is the context in which we perceive truth about loss, death, and resurrection, and we seek to find comfort and impart it to others. Our perception of truth, our reception of comfort and hope, and our ministry of imparting it to others are all done in *participation* or fellowship with God.

But does this mean that only Christians can know any truth about humanity and loss and the experience of grief? No. God has also revealed himself through creation. This *general* revelation is accessible to all human beings. This involves the intellectual human response to the macro-observation that the universe is massive, powerful, ordered, and beautiful, and that there must a God, though the latter conclusion is suppressed by the fallen heart. Paul refers to this in his letter to the Romans 1:19–20: *"what may be known about God is plain to them, because God has made it plain to them. For since the creation of the world God's invisible qualities—his eternal power and divine nature—have been clearly seen, being understood from what has been made, so that people are without excuse."*

But by extrapolation, this also includes all truth accessible through all the micro-discoveries of the sciences. All humans are made in the image of God, and whether they are Christian, Hindu, Buddhist, or atheist, they have been given capacity to respond to sensory evidence and to use reason in garnering and reflecting on evidence gained. They also have the capacity to be self-reflective and to have self-understanding, to work and to pursue shalom in the world. Thus, the field of human psychology (along with other sciences, both hard and soft) has important truth to contribute to our understanding of grief and loss. There is truth to be discovered in the work of Freud, Rogers, Fairbairn, and so on.

Of course, these scientists are part of a humanity that, according to special revelation, is fallen. Since the first human person disobeyed God, all human beings have been spiritually and relationally off kilter. The fallen condition of humanity does not erase the image of God, but it has defaced or marred it. Thus, our attempts as a fallen human race to pursue work, create technology, and build a better world are adversely affected by our alienation from God, from ourselves, from our neighbor, and from creation. Our denial of God ("the death of God") in the modern era, or at least our consigning him to the private realm of faith and values, means that although we can still process scientific truth, we don't integrate it philosophically into a worldview—or better, a heart-view—that includes God. Scientists of the naturalist persuasion, including psychological and social scientists, insist that science is the realm of pure reason, in which there can be no room for the God-hypothesis. But as noted above, the reality is that objectivity and answers based on reason are only possible when we have isolated the issue. Science can answer the "small" questions about how the atoms within certain molecules are spatially arranged, or what DNA sequence is present in the human genome. However, it cannot answer big questions about the cosmos and its meaning without invoking faith or prejudice for or against a God hypothesis. Furthermore, philosophers like Michael Polanyi[8] have shown science itself to be just as subject to faith assumptions as other disciplines. Science is practically inseparable from some metaphysical commitments. As John Lennox indicates, "the Enlightenment ideal of the coolly rational scientific observer, completely independent, free of all preconceived theories, prior philosophical, ethical and religious commitments, doing investigations and coming to dispassionate, unbiased conclusions that constitute absolute truth, is nowadays regarded by serious philosophers of science (and, indeed, most scientists) as a simplistic myth." He goes on to say, "In common with the rest of humanity, scientists have preconceived ideas, indeed, worldviews that they bring to bear on every situation."[9]

Furthermore, the denial of God and the self-oriented streak that characterizes our fallenness (we all are turned in on ourselves) leads us to seek work and wealth for our own selfish ends to the neglect of the other, and to pursue industry in a way that has raped our environment instead of nurturing it. With respect to psychology, a fundamental assumption of the Freudian approach was the denial of God, and the assertion that God

8. See Polanyi, *Tacit Dimension.*

9. Lennox, *God's Undertaker*, 33. Lennox does not take the extreme position that all science is therefore a "totally subjective and arbitrary social construct," as suggested by some thinkers of postmodern persuasion. Instead he proposes that science is done in "critical realist" fashion.

was the projection of the human psyche's desire for the perfect father. Thus, the discerning Christian seeks for any truth she may find in Freud's great legacy, as long as it does not contradict first-order theology—but she will also be aware of areas where an anti-God bias may have skewed Freud's reflections. She will keep an eye towards the fact that Freud, though valued for his contribution, has been surpassed in the development of the field of psychological and psychotherapeutic understanding. Thus, while special revelation is infallible, Freud is not.

What follows here, then, is an attempt to reflect a critically realistic, trinitarian, integrative, and encyclopedic account of the nature of grief and grief recovery, one in which we will try to bring the best insights of the psychology of grief into conversation with the insights of first-order Christian theology about the human person and psyche . . . around the theme of grief-sharing.

chapter 5

The Source and Nature of Grief

INSIGHTS FROM TRINITARIAN THEOLOGY—*MODELING*

It might be stating the glaringly obvious, but *loss* often causes us to feel *lost*. When I experienced the loss of Sharon, I felt lost. How could I not? This is not mushy sentimentality. Her soul was intertwined in mine, and mine in hers, for a long time. So when she went, I lost a piece of myself. So did our kids. Etched into my memory is the first dinner we had as a family alone, two days after Sharon died. I thought to lighten the sense of shock and loss by taking Martyn and Heather out to dinner, to their favorite pizza restaurant, Me'n'Eds. It was a mistake. We sat at the table, none of us knowing what to say yet each trying to be brave for the others' sake, holding back the tears. We were utterly lost, as a family and as persons. The absence of the fourth person in the circle screamed "loss." The poignant absence of she who was the emotional center of our family. Our reference point. She was deeply part of us. Now gone. Yes, we were lost.

Four months later, back teaching at Regent College, I had this sense of lostness accentuated in a very tangible way. After class on the first day, pleased that I had kept it together for lectures, I dumped my briefcase into the back seat, jumped into the driving seat, and reached for the cell phone to call Sharon, tell her about my day and let her know that I was just leaving. Of course, it suddenly dawned on me she wasn't there. No use ringing 604 3247292. She wasn't going to answer. I broke down and cried. Who could give me that sense of belonging, that reference point, that emotional steadiness and wisdom?

Though less acute, this sense of lostness persists eight years later. I am assuming she will *always* be part of me in some sense, that any virtue she helped to form in me will remain, but that the pieces of myself that were lost will not return. My heart has by grace been given the capacity to love another person, and to allow that person in, and to become reintegrated in some way. But grief is a consequence of taking the risk of sharing our souls. It is in the very nature of human personhood to do that. We are interpersonal, communal, relational persons. Our personhood is constituted by other persons and our relations with them. This accounts for the gravity of our losses, both for the one who is dying and for those who are left. Relationality with God and other human persons also enables us to recover and be reintegrated. The nature of grief is that it is, in its very essence, "grief-sharing," a consequence of being interpersonal. It comes from sharing in the life of others—from sharing our selves. In a broken world where death still exists, we run the risk of the loss of the other who is part of our interpersonal self. And that hurts. We feel lost.

In considering the motif of *grief-sharing*, then, we first recognize that this concept is important because the nature of grief is profoundly related to the relational and personal nature of human beings. There are a number of theories about the nature of loss and grief, but the most helpful lens for understanding the power of the grief response is a relational and personal one: the reality of the interpersonal nature of the human self. This is an anthropological insight from trinitarian theology, which we consider in this chapter. It is also consonant with insights from psychology and in a particular way, attachment theory—something we will major on in chapter 7.

Explaining Grief on the Basis of Interpersonal Self: God as Trinity as the Window for Understanding Human Persons . . . and Their Grief

Loss cannot be understood until we grasp the wonder of human *personhood*. It is important to grasp that persons have an irreducible, unique identity, *and* that they are interpersonal and profoundly relational and communal. The classic Western idea of humans as self-made intellects, or even psychologically self-realized individuals, is ill-conceived. Equally misguided is the polar opposite of atomism, the notion of collectivism—that is, of society viewed as a collection of undifferentiated persons who sacrifice identity for the sake of the state or the whole. A gospel understanding of humans is that they reflect their triune Creator, who is three interpenetrated persons, mutually internal to one another in a unity of essence and communion.

For the Trinity, *communion* and *persons* are equiprimal. That is, there has never been and will never be a divine person without the presence of the other divine persons in a perfect communion. Each is completely in the other, and each animates the other. Yet each has an irreducible identity uncompromised by the communion. This social doctrine of the Trinity is, I believe, the correct one,[1] based on biblical grounding, and especially the Johannine insights into the Trinity.[2] It is also based on economical con

1. As opposed to the psychological model of the Trinity, which has illustrative strengths but is built too heavily on a "from below" anthropological premise and stresses unity at the expense of personhood. For a critique of the psychological analogy, see my work on the Trinity in Edwards, in *The Life of God in Jonathan Edwards*. As noted there, the idea that a social understanding of the Trinity was derived from the Cappadocian fathers, and a psychological one from Augustine, is disputed. Augustine most likely was in full accord with the Cappadocians. However, it can be said in fairness that Augustine's psychological analogy, intended for pastoral illustration, became a popular one in the Western tradition, leading to a neglect of personhood. Miroslav Volf's observation of a correlation between the views of personhood and community in the three great ecclesiastical traditions—Orthodoxy, Catholicism, and the Free Churches—and the prevailing view of the Trinity in each, is valid and instructive. See Volf, *After Our Likeness*. Common to all these traditions is a stress on the relational nature of persons. The Catholic tradition represented by Ratzinger stresses communion or relations to such an extent that the persons of the Trinity are spoken of as "relations" (relations *as* persons), rather than as persons-in-relation. This translates into a de-emphasis on individual faith and emphasis on the organized unity of the church. The social Trinity has come under fire recently (see, for example, Holmes, *Quest for the Trinity*) but, properly understood, it seems to accord best with what we have seen in the personal revelation of Jesus.

2. John 10:38; 14:10–11; 17:21–26; and 1 John 2:24 speak of the Father and the Son *being* each "in the other." Other passages speak of a perichoresis of *action* (John 4:34; 5:30, 38; 8:29 with respect to mutual *mission*; 3:34; 7:16; 8:26 with respect to mutual *speaking*, both of which flow out of a relationship of perfect love [3:35; 10:17], knowledge [10:14] and mutual glorification [16:14; 17:22, 24]). I am grateful to John Witvliet for this summary (Witvliet, "Doctrine of the Trinity," 256). With respect to the complete mutuality of the persons of the Son and the Spirit, this may be summed up in Stephen Williams's comment: "The greatness of divine unity is magnified when we think how the Spirit comes upon the Son and the Son sends the Spirit in undivided concord and fellowship" (Williams, "The Trinity and Other Religions," 35). A Johannine text that reflects the perichoretic relationship between the Son and the Spirit is John 14:18, where, speaking in the context of his ascension, Jesus promises the coming of the Spirit, the result of which enables him to say, "*I will not leave you as orphans, I will come to you.*" Shortly after, Jesus speaks about the giving of the Spirit that will enable the disciples to both have insight into trinitarian reality, and to *participate* in the life of the Trinity: "*On that day you will realize that I am in my Father, and you are in me, and I am in you*" (John 14:20). The presence of the Spirit in believing persons would be tantamount to the presence of the Son (and indeed, the Father, v. 23!): *I am in you*. But this is because the Son first became one with us, by the Spirit, at the incarnation: *you are in Me*. All this arises from the eternal

siderations; that is, based on the historical revelation of God the Father in the persons of the incarnate Son and the given Holy Spirit. Our best insight into the Trinity is surely in Jesus, truly a *person*, and therefore the proper grounding for good analogy.

There is scarcely a better summation of the reality and relevant crucial terms of the doctrine of the Trinity than that expressed by Cornelius Plantinga:

> The holy Trinity is a transcendent society or community of three fully divine entities: the Father, the Son and the Holy Spirit or Paraclete. These three are wonderfully unified by their common divinity, by the possession by each of the whole divine essence— including, for instance, the properties of everlastingness, and sublimely great knowledge, love, and glory. They are also unified by their common historical-redemptive purpose, revelation, and work. Their knowledge and love are directed not only to their creatures, but also primordially and archetypally to each other. The Trinity is thus a zestful, wondrous community of divine light, love, joy, mutuality, and verve.
>
> Each member is a person, a distinct person, but scarcely an *individual* or *separate* person. For in the divine life there is no isolation, no insulation, no secretiveness, no fear of being transparent to another. Hence there may be penetrating, inside knowledge of the other *as other*, but as co-other, loved other, fellows. Father, Son, and Spirit are "members of one another" to a superlative and exemplary degree.[3]

The Path from God to Humanity

Of course, making any analogy between who God is and who we are as human beings needs to be done with great care. It is good to ask why the statement that God is Trinity, a statement about God (theology proper), can be used to provide insight into the identity (theological anthropology) and the ideals (ethics) of human existence. Alistair McFadyen has warned of the dangers of analogies made in too facile a manner, and he has pointed out that "*how* one moves from talking about the Triune being of God to human being is decisively important."[4] This highlights the need for consis-

---

communion and covenant of the Father and the Son by the Spirit.

3. Plantinga, "Threeness/Oneness Problem," 50.

4. McFadyen, "Trinity and Human Individuality," 10–18. Emphasis added. See also

tency with biblical revelation, and the preservation of the transcendence of God, as well as the appropriate use of terms.

For example, human persons cannot reflect *perfectly* either the personhood-in-relation of God nor the completeness of relationality of the discrete persons (communion). The term "community," in my opinion, ought not to be used of the Divine being, but only for the social existence of human beings that reflects the Trinity. Rather, the oneness of the persons of the Trinity is best expressed as "communion." "Community" seems to suggest a gathering of three individuals and therefore tritheism (three Gods), rather than Trinity (three completely internally mutual persons). It is an appropriate term for human persons, who reflect and even approach likeness to the divine model but can never achieve it. Similarly, the term "coinherence" or "perichoresis," which refers to the interpenetration of the divine persons in both their being and their doing—the fact that each is fully in the other and animated by the other, such that the unity of the Godhead is a function of these relations—should be reserved for God alone. The interpenetration of human persons, in marriage for example, can only be an echo of this at best.

Yet we *are* the image of this God. We *do* echo divine reality. The view of the interpersonal self as constituting the image of God is profoundly consonant with the view of humanity presented in the biblical story. The first chapter of Genesis, which contains the beginning of the story, contains the account of God creating human beings in the divine image. The foundation of the prototypical human self is "the internalized response of the significant other," though in this case it is the significant "Other." The primal foundation of the human self is knowledge of God. The prevalent view throughout the history of scholarly Christian tradition is that the image of God (*imago Dei*) is a *relational* concept. That is, it is the capacity given by God to humanity to be in relationship with him ("*in the image of God created he them*") in an intimate and covenantal way. T. F. Torrance interestingly notes that *God* is the primary actor when it comes to human beings bearing his image: "It is, fundamentally, God who does the beholding of the image. *He images Himself in man*."[5] Because of this, by God's grace, each person is able to be in relationship to him, and then in relationship with fellow humans, in a manner that reflects equality and otherness ("*male and female created he them*"), and to be in relationship with creation, as God's

---

McFadyen, *Call to Personhood*.

5. T. F. Torrance, *Calvin's Doctrine of Man*, 42. Emphasis added.

representatives in the temple of his creation. *Imago Dei*—or in light of all revelation, *imago trinitatis*—is the communal nature of persons who are mutually loving and self-giving. There are other opinions about the nature of the *imago Dei*—the capacity of humans to reason and self-reflect (the structural view), and the God-given ability and duty to be stewards of creation (the functional view)—but both of these are dependent on the fundamental relational reality that human beings are persons-in-relation with God, each other, and creation. We are therefore an *analogy* of the relational and personal God.[6] Thus we are remarkably unique persons, and at the same time, we are persons who are profoundly interpersonal. Though we cannot ever be completely mutually internal to one another, we are interdependent on one another. We know a measure of mutual interpenetration. We are able to inter-animate one another.

The validity of *"bridging concepts"* that allow us to say something about human identity and ideals on the basis of who God is, as proposed by Christoph Schwöbel and Colin Gunton,[7] has been helpful. John Witvliet, drawing on their work, has suggested that these bridging concepts are of

6. The relationship between divine and human personhood is not univocal but analogous. For Barth, the nexus of the relations of the person of Christ as the Son of God within the Trinity, and his relationship as man with all humanity, expresses the appropriate analogy between God and humanity by a technical term, "the analogy of relations" (*analogia relationis*). As Barth states, it "follows that the person who corresponds to, and reflects, the being of God bears the stamp of God's own dynamic character. Each human person then is destined to be in relation: to be I and Thou. I implies Thou, and Thou refers back to I. I and Thou are not coincidental or incidental but essentially proper to the concept of 'man' . . . ." Barth, *CD* III/2, 248. Despite the limitations of Barth's doctrine of the Trinity (God as one divine Subject, persons as "modes of being"), the *analogia relationis* is a critical concept in Barth's anthropology and a major contribution to human thought. This was the notion that when speaking of human persons we must speak of relations, not merely of being. Another way of saying this was that he viewed as analogous the correspondence between the humanity and deity of Christ, and a correspondence between human love and divine love. Barth preferred this over the Thomistic *analogia entis* (analogy of being), foundational to much Catholic theology. It represents a paradigm shift in that it suggests that being and relations are simultaneous to one another, and that being is inseparable from the relations that constitute a human person's existence. Barth demonstrates in a profound way the relationship between the divine Personhood within the Trinity and human personhood, without confusion as to the essence of divinity and humanity. It is an analogy of relations, not essence, and it is a relationality couched from beginning to end in the grace of God.

7. See Schwöbel, *Trinitarian Theology*. See also Schwöbel and Gunton, *Persons Divine and Human*, and T. F. Torrance's tightly argued exposition of the "onto-relational" understanding of personhood in both God and humanity in T. F. Torrance, *Reality and Evangelical Theology*.

two main kinds: those based on the idea of a *model*, that is, that human existence models divine existence; and those based on the idea of the *participation* of human persons and communities in the divine communion.[8] If we can carefully but legitimately think of the Trinity as the model for human being and doing, that is for anthropology and ethics, this will perhaps be inspiring. However, if we use the bridging concept of model only, we will be destined for despair. The only reason we model the Triune God is that we are in relationship with him, such that we participate in his life, in his personhood, in his communion! Imaging divine life in ways that give insight into the socio-ethical existence of humanity, and specifically in ways that help us understand grief—as this has been expounded by trinitarian theologians—is valuable. However, apart from the great gospel reality of participation in divine life and love, this imaging would be impossible, and the comfort gained from this perspective would be minimal. These bridging concepts absolutely go together.

The very concept of humanity being in the image of God, going back to Adam and Eve, was contingent upon their relationship with God—their participation in divine life—through the mediation of Christ. John Calvin surmised that even the first Adam, before the fall, imaged God only because he was in participation in the pre-incarnate Christ, as Clement Wen confirms:

> Easy as it might be to recognize Christ as "Mediator" only *after* the fall (by way of the Incarnation), Calvin saw that "Even if man had remained free from all stain, his condition would have been too lowly for him to reach God without a Mediator" (II.12.1). As such, he maintained that it was *Christ* who was our Mediator *even before the fall*, and that this truth was by virtue of the fact that even from the beginning, "Christ was set over angels and men as their Head," as He was "the first-born of all creation [Col 1:15]" (II.12.4).[9] "Hence," says Calvin, "whatever excellence was *engraved* upon Adam [was] derived from the fact that he approached the glory of his Creator *through the only-begotten Son*" (II.12.6; emphasis mine). Thus, only by way of *participation in Christ* was Adam a "mirror" of God's glory (II.12.6). Only by way of Adam's dynamic "union with Christ" *did God behold Himself* (which is to say: *did God "image" Himself*) in Adam. For, even before the fall, "both angels as well as men were *united to God by [Christ's] grace*

---

8. Witvliet, "Doctrine of the Trinity," 259–63.

9. See Calvin, "How Christ is the Mediator," 12–13.

so that they would remain uncorrupted."[10] . . . Adam and Eve were continually reminded that their very lives, *their very ability to "image" God, was utterly dependent upon communion (κοινωνία) with God.*[11]

Julie Canlis, in a similar vein, states with respect to Calvin's participatory understanding of anthropology that "God does not give us things [e.g. 'image'] that would then function without him; *their very character demands communion.*"[12]

The fall did not erase the image of God, for God continued to love and view humanity. Our receptors were damaged, however, and the image in fallen humanity is now defaced and distorted. Humanity did not cease, metaphysically speaking, to be persons-in-relation. But persons are spiritually alienated, subject to death, morally fallen, and emotionally broken, and their relations are always in need of reconciliation. Through the coming of the Son of God into the world to become human and be the ultimate image of the invisible God for us, the true and last Adam, and by the operation of God's grace in our lives when we come into union with him by faith, the image of God is gradually restored to fullness. The very heart of the Christian life is the loving contemplation of the glory of God (2 Cor 3:18), in order that from one degree of glory to another, the fullness of humanity as triune-God-reflection is restored. Humans can love again: love God, love neighbor, love creation.[13] In this era, death still prevails—it has been defeated by the decisive victory of the death and resurrection of the primal representative of humanity, the last Adam, Christ, but it is "yet to be destroyed" finally at his second coming. Therefore in this era, losses of loved ones mean losses of an integral part of our selves. This chapter expresses why that is so at a theological level. Essentially, we are deeply interpenetrated persons who reflect the God who created us. The stunning reality of being like God makes us prone to shock and grief when we lose loved ones! It is also, however, comforting to know that the God who made

10. Calvin, "How Christ is the Mediator," 12; emphasis original.

11. Wen, "Monergistic Theme," 90. References in parentheses refer to Calvin's Institutes.

12. Canlis, *Calvin's Ladder*, 78; emphasis added.

13. Theologian Hendrikus Berkhof, in his correlation between the social nature of God and humans, stated, "Human life is, after all, living in relationship. We are human in and through our relationship to the world around us, to our fellow human beings, our job, societal structures, culture, science, nature." In a manner that reflects Barth's anthropology, he adds, "Humanness is always fellow-humanness.' Berkhof, *Christian Faith*, 344.

us this way is in relationship with us . . . always, and even especially when we go through the deep waters of suffering, comforting us and slowly re-forming us. The modeling and the participating go together. I want to say a little more about each.

The Modeling Bridge

Model Made by the Relational God

The "bridging concept" of the *modeling* of human personhood and com-munity after divine personhood and communion is present in a great deal of trinitarian theology since Karl Barth.[14] As Witvliet says, the "common thread in these writings is the notion that an entity is defined by its rela-tionships with other entities, and that persons are defined by relationships with other persons." Barth's sense of this is reflected, for example, when he states, "I am in encounter with the other who is in the same way as I am. . . . I cannot posit myself without coming up against the self-positing of the other. . . . [T]he minimal definition of our humanity, or humanity gener-ally, must be that it is the being of man in encounter, and in this sense the determination of man as a being with the other men."[15] His use of the term "co-humanity" for humanity was evidence of this. Jürgen Moltmann was another key figure in developing this analogy. He spoke of humanity living in a "world of growing interdependencies," and he encouraged "thinking in networks and milieus"[16] rather than as isolated entities. He spoke of being a person as "existing-in-relationship."[17] He states,

14. Three brief examples (cited in Witvliet, "Doctrine of the Trinity," 260), among many we could cite, will suffice to illustrate this. Peter Van Inwagen asserts that "the love we have for each other will be a restored image of the love that the Persons of the Trinity have for one another" (Van Inwagen, "They are not Three," 242). Lesslie Newbigin contends that "a trinitarian understanding of God corresponds to this vision of *koinōnia* as the goal of human existence" (Newbigin, "Trinity as Public Truth," 7). Most eloquently, Wolfhart Pannenberg states, "The correspondence between the image of God in human beings and the Trinitarian life of God is in fact fulfilled in the human community and specifically in the community of God's kingdom" (Pannenberg, *Anthropology in Theo-logical Perspective*, 531). In an ecumenical document, he further writes, "The movement towards community is a reflection of the communion which exists in God himself. The deepest aspiration of human life corresponds to the dynamics of the life of the Trinity" (Pannenberg, "Reconciling Power of the Trinity," 84).

15. Barth, *CD III/2*, 246–47.

16. Moltmann, *Trinity and the Kingdom*, 19, ix.

17. Ibid., 172, ix.

To be alive means existing in relationship with other people and things. Life is communication in communion. And conversely, isolation and lack of relationship means death for all living things, and dissolution even for elementary particles. So if we want to understand what is real as real, and what is living as living, we have to know it in its own primal and individual community, in its relationship, interconnections and surroundings.[18]

A key argument for the validity of the modeling bridge is the historical legacy of the term "person" and its meaning. The true legacy of the term "person" is not Western, Cartesian individualism (I think, therefore, I am), but the fourth-century trinitarian debates (I am because you are), in which it became clear that by sheer divine grace, human personhood was analogous to Divine trinitarian personhood. Alan Torrance strongly contends this is the case. He affirms John Zizioulas's inversion of the Western category of substance, with its individualistic connotations, when applied to the concept of the person. Whereas Boethius famously argued, "*persona est substantia individua rationabilis naturae*" (the person is an individual substance with a rational nature), Torrance states that "Zizioulas translates the Latin *substantia* into the Greek *hypostasis* and then introduces a wordplay to make his point." And this is Zizioulas's point: "The person is a unique kind of being which has his or her *hypostasis* in *ekstasis*, that is, precisely in its noncircumscribability. The person is a uniquely Christian category, and the West has lost this vision characteristic of patristic (Cappadocian) thought.[19] At the most fundamental level, he suggests, *person* is to be conceived in such a way that relations are fundamental to their being. When they are conceived in terms of the monadic individualistic categories characteristic of much Western Christianity, the most fundamental feature of their being is lost."[20]

The individualism of the West has needed to be rescued by trinitarian reality. With a focus on rational faculties, "In Descartes and his successors we have the individualist, which collapses so easily into the collectivist."[21]

18. Moltmann, *God in Creation*, 3.

19. Wolfhart Pannenberg has also indicated that the meaning of the term "person" for a human person gained its meaning in Western culture in the context of the articulation of "persons" in God. (See Pannenberg, *Basic Questions*, 228–32). We owe this debt actually to the Eastern fathers, the Cappadocians, whose discoveries were inherited by the West.

20. Alan Torrance, "On Deriving Ought From Is," 189.

21. See ibid., 193–94, and Gunton, *Promise of Trinitarian Theology*, 87–92.

In his account in *The Promise of Trinitarian Theology*, Colin Gunton examines an altogether "different ontology" from the Cartesian one, that of John MacMurray. Gunton finds "the first evidence for a more relational view of the matter, that we truly find ourselves neither as individuals nor as parts of collectives, but as persons in free relations to each other."[22] Gunton's resistance to either absolutization—individualism or collectivism—leaves him defending a middle ground that preserves relational and personal ontological integrity as essential constituents of personhood. MacMurray is important, Gunton suggests, because this unique ontology seems to arise out of an implicitly trinitarian reflection. Trinitarian reflection, as described above, is one of Gunton's key points of emphasis, and other thinkers whom he appreciates with regard to *imago* theology are all marked by this commitment.[23]

But how do we bridge the divine-human divide without confusing God and humanity? We affirm, with Alan Torrance, the "radical and dynamic continuity between the divine and the human that is the event of Christ."[24] Thus, emphatically, the analogy or modeling is grounded not in univocity but in Christ, by way of the *analogia relationis*. Oliver O'Donovan has confirmed this specifically Christological grounding of the analogy. He writes,

> Christian thinkers of the patristic period, in the course of their debates about the Trinity and the person of Christ, brought the term "person" into theological, and eventually into philosophical, currency in order to escape from an impasse created by classical patterns of thought about human individuality. They had inherited from the ancient world the conception that individuality resided in "reason" (*nous*) or "soul" (*psyche*). But when these genetic categories were applied to the individuality of Christ, they led to a range of unthinkable options: either Christ, by virtue of being both God and man, was two individuals; or, being one individual, he did not have all the attributes of humanity and divinity; or (closest to the classical world) the highest attributes in man were anyway divine. Their solution to the impasse was to draw the sharp distinction between the concepts of "person" and "nature" famously maintained in the Chalcedonian definition. In speaking of Christ

22. Gunton, *Promise of Trinitarian Theology*, 92.

23. Of special importance for Gunton was Coleridge, and the trinitarian foundations reflected in several of his works (see ibid., 98–100).

24. Alan Torrance, *Persons in Communion*, 209.

as "one person in two natures" the Council of Chalcedon used the term "person" (*hypostasis*) to represent the non-generic principle of individual existence, and "nature" to represent the complex of attributes, divine or human, which constitute the generic distinctness of divinity and humanity. Through the influence of Boethius' Fifth Tractate upon philosophers this conception became generalized from the unique person of Christ to all persons. Thus the human individual was conceived not merely as a concretization of his human attributes, but as a bearer of them: he is not merely a "chip off the old block" of total humanity, but *someone who is human*. This perception has its roots in the biblical understanding of individual vocation. Prior to those events which bring our humanity to being, we are called by God: "Before I formed you in the womb I knew you" (Jer 1:5).[25]

Model as the Relational Human

There is a second dimension of the image-bearing nature of the human persons of Genesis 1. They are not just interpersonal human beings because the personal God is in relationship with them, though this is definitive of the very concept of the image. They also reflect his own inherently interpersonal nature *in their nature*. By this I refer to the fact that in the description of the image-imparting event, by which God pronounces and constitutes the two prototypical humans as his image on earth, the text immediately states "*male and female created He them*" (Gen 1:27). "*So God created mankind in his own image*" is followed by a clarifying phrase that asserts both the *plurality* of the humans made in his image (*in the image of God he created them*) and the *differentiation* within the plurality (*male and female he created them*). It is apparent that the image of God is reflected in two sub-types of human persons, who constitute the image together, as two persons with differentiation, not sameness. Genderedness is proper to the image of God. It is as two *people in relationship* that they image God. It is as two *equal* but *different* persons in relationship that they image God. There is a created givenness about the interpersonal nature of persons, and there is a givenness about the part that gender plays in that interpersonal nature. When the equality and the differences in gender are honored in humanity, God is imaged well—for God, as the fullness of revelation reveals, is a

---

25. O'Donovan, *Resurrection and the Moral Order*, 238. Emphasis original.

relational God in three persons who are equally divine and equal in honor, and yet who have irreducible identity as Father, Son, and Holy Spirit.

It is important to note that it is not just married persons who image the interpersonal nature of divine persons. All human persons are interpersonal. Ray Anderson expresses it this way: "There is at least an intentional correspondence . . . between the intrinsic plurality of human beings as constituted male and female and the being of God in whose likeness and image this plurality exists. . . . Quite clearly the imago is not totally present in the form of individual humanity, but more completely as co-humanity. It is thus quite natural and expected that God himself is also a 'we.'"[26] The joy of being sexual beings (quite apart from having sex) is that it is a consequence of creation in the image of the Triune God of grace; it drives us to know God, and it drives us to be other-oriented, to know friends, to relate as equals. It drives us out of ourselves and into relationship with others, but it drives us to do so as persons with our own distinct personhood, of which gender is a significant part. The mystery of contemplative, healthy sexuality is thoroughly grounded in the mystery of trinitarian theology! James Houston expressed it this way: "To know the Triune God is to act like Him, in self-giving, in inter-dependence, and in boundless love."[27] Maleness and femaleness were essential for humanity to bear the image of a triune, eternally intimate God. To be an artistic expression of God we needed to be male and female, which takes us beyond the biology and psychology of sex to its spirituality.

The design of God in creating the sexual drive was not just procreation. It was to drive humanity to seek him, and to seek community, to move us outside of ourselves. Similarly, Paul Stevens states that "It takes both sexes in relation to each other to express God in a human metaphor. Neither the fall into sin nor the substantial redemption accomplished by Christ alters the essential truth that male and female are *together* the image of God. Therefore God-likeness is a social reality. True spirituality is interpersonal, relational. Relationships are pathways to God."[28]

Thus, we may conclude that all human persons are interpersonal and therefore prone, when loss occurs, to grief experienced as the loss of something of themselves. This is true especially of those we are close to.

26. Anderson, *On Being Human*, 73.

27. Houston, lectures in "Trinitarian Spirituality," Regent College, 1989, cited in R. Paul Stevens, *Disciplines of a Hungry Heart*, 73.

28. Stevens, *Disciplines of a Hungry Heart*, 68, 69.

Friendship has been described as the highest form of human love; one reason for this is that the complications of sex do not intrude. The greatest biblical illustration of deep friendship love is described between the Old Testament king David and his friend Jonathan. When Jonathan died, David grieved deeply. His words capture the grief of a lost friend: "I *grieve* for you Jonathan, my brother, you were very dear to me. Your love for me was wonderful, more wonderful than that of women" (2 Sam 1:26).

Even when we do not know people well, we can sense that a piece of ourselves has been taken. As I have been writing this section, the tragic news of the suicide of Robin Williams has been announced. I did not know him personally, but because of my exposure to his humor and his acting personae, and my awareness of his struggle with bipolar depression, I identified with him at some level. A little piece of many people died when he died.

Now marriage is a particular example of what it means that persons are interpersonal, and that they image God. I have stressed already that marriage is not essential to the image of God. That is, genderedness—not marriage—is what is affirmed in Genesis 1 as constituting image-bearing. The fact that Jesus was not married is supreme justification of this notion and of the fact that one does not need to have genital sex to be fulfilled as a human person.[29] Marriage, in which sexual intimacy and intercourse are permitted within the safety of covenant commitment between a man and a woman, signifies a different aspect of God's being and love. Within covenant, sex is *expressed* as a consummation of covenant ("*the two shall become one flesh*," Gen 2:24), which involves a *public* act of leaving and a commitment to permanent covenant union. As Grenz and Bell have indicated, both single and married people reflect the love of God, though in different ways. The state of singleness represents the inclusivity of the love of God, while marriage reflects the exclusivity of his covenant love towards his own people.[30] The "one flesh" statement quoted above is highly evocative of the Trinity! There is a oneness of more than one . . . two persons

29. Richard Rohr comments on life as a single monk in this manner: "God seemingly had to take all kinds of risks in order that we would not miss the one thing necessary: we are called and even driven out of ourselves by an almost insatiable appetite so that we would never presume that we were self-sufficient. It is so important that we know that we are incomplete, needy, and essentially social that God had to create a life-force within us that would not be silenced—not until 10 minutes after we were dead, they told us novices!" Rohr, "An Appetite For Wholeness," 30.

30. See Grenz and Bell, *Betrayal of Trust*.

mysteriously become one, with a oneness of communion that is as real as the oneness of the one true God. This helps to explain the depth of the grief that is experienced by a bereaved man or woman, who for years has known both friendship and intimacy at every level.

Therefore, when I lost Sharon it is not surprising that I felt as though a large piece of my soul had been ripped out. We were interpenetrated in every human way possible. We had shared history for twenty-eight years, twenty-seven as a married couple. She had prayed for me through every sermon, and in every new stage of our lives we had gone together through the ups and downs of discernment processes. We laughed a lot, and sometimes she was laughing with me, and if I tripped over something, she laughed uproariously at me. I was deeply dependent on her in so many ways. Emotionally, of course. And for wisdom about practical things in life and ministry—like when to visit someone in the hospital and when to stay away, and what to say when I saw them. Yes, we modeled the Trinity in a small way. This was delightful. But it also made us prone—in a fallen world, a world of cancer—to great loss and great grief. Mine after she was taken; hers in the days leading to her death. Perhaps the most indelible memory I have during the whole process of her illness and dying was on the day when we discovered there was now no chemotherapy available, and that Sharon was going to have to go into the palliative ward. Our son was at school in another city, and telling him by phone was awful enough, but seeing Sharon tell Heather in person that it didn't look like she was going to make it, and seeing them hugging together in bed and crying, seemed too much for me to bear. I can only imagine that it was even worse for Sharon.

From these modeling realities, we may draw two conclusions related to what persons are, and why and how persons grieve. The first conclusion affirms that human persons have *irreducible identity*. No one experience of grief is the same as another. "I know what you're going through" can never be entirely true. Each experience of grief is unique, and so is the way it is experienced. But secondly, the fact that we are formed as *interpersonal selves* or *relational persons*, interdependent and interanimated, makes sense of how deeply loss affects us, the shock element in grief and the depth of the grieving process by which we gradually let go and are re-integrated.

I confess I am still fathoming how much we were interpersonal, ensconced in one another, even eight years on from the death of my beloved Sharon. I hardly knew who I was apart from who she was. She was complementary to me in so many, many ways. She was a solid rock of stability. I grew up in three different countries and lived in too many houses to count. I have a Heinz 57 varieties accent, with the chief influences being Scottish, Zimbabwean, and Canadian. I can relate well to people of many cultures, but sometimes I feel like a chameleon and wonder who I really am! Sharon did not have any of these identity struggles. She grew up in one home in Prestwick, Scotland, until she was twenty-five, and she spoke broad Scotts even after close to thirty years in Canada. She knew who she was. Somehow I gained stability from her stability and identity from her identity. And then she was gone.

Sharon was the emotional center of our home and of my own emotional well-being. Sometimes, I know, this was not just healthy interdependence but merged into co-dependence, blurring my identity in inappropriate ways. She could call me on that well. I have suffered from depression most of my adult life. Sharon could comfort me like no other and tell me she admired my courage in working through it, but she could also scold me like no other if I lapsed into self-pity. I take myself way too seriously. Sharon could burst that bubble like no other. Sharon, like many other Scots, did not treat lowly paupers and lofty CEOs or prime ministers any differently. They were just people to her. People with need. I learned to overcome my fear of big-named people through her. And then she was gone.

Yes, the loss of a person is a loss to ourselves. We have lost a piece of our selves. Redemption will come when that person is restored into our communion, and especially when the fullness of our union with Christ will be realized. The personal and communal nature of God gives insight into grief—but also into its resolution, as subsequent chapters will show.

Another way of seeing grief, which is underpinned by an interpersonal view of the human person, is grief *as a process of realization*. This is consonant with the thought that grief is shock-thaw. It is the new expression of feelings as we slowly thaw out from shock and gradually come to terms with the full impact of our loss.

chapter 6

The Source and Nature of Grief

INSIGHTS FROM TRINITARIAN THEOLOGY—

PARTICIPATING

The Participation Bridge

HAVING LOOKED AT HOW our imaging or *modeling* of the Trinity gives insight into our nature and vulnerability as human persons, I want to emphasize that this modeling is only possible through our *participation* in the life and love of the Triune God. This will illumine further our nature as persons and open up resources for dealing with our losses and grief. Alistair McFadyen is correct to emphasize that apart from participation, the idea of broken human persons in broken human churches and cities and nations can seem oppressive:

> Dangling a model of perfect community above the heads of fallen human beings does nothing to empower or enable us to reconstitute ourselves of our relationships; all it gives anyone with an appreciation of the brokenness of human persons, relationships and societies is a sense of guilt and hopelessness.[1]

By contrast, McFadyen insists "what is needed is not a model, but the communication of the energies of true relation and individuation from the Triune being of God." Perhaps he overstates to make his point. It seems to me the model is important and necessary. But he rightly wishes to emphasize that though the inspiration may come from the model, the source and power for imaging God comes from dynamic interaction with the personal

1. McFadyen, "Trinity and Human Individuality," 13–14.

61

and relational God with whom humans are in relationship by grace. The imperatives of modeling would be impossible and cruel if there were not first the indicatives of the gospel, drawing us into union with Christ by the Spirit. McFadyen tersely expresses the essence of the point of this chapter, and the grounding of a relationship among trinitarian theology, attachment theory, and other relational theories in psychology: "Human individuality and sociality become what they properly are by virtue of their dynamic interaction with the trinitarian God."[2] As Witvliet has said, "In McFadyen's language, divine relationality is not so much (or not only) a model to imitate but a reality in which human beings are invited to participate."[3] This invitation and capacity of humans to participate in the life and relations of God is one of sheer grace. Bruce McCormack, interpreting Karl Barth in this regard, has commented that Barth's *analogia relationis* is very important. He also offers the comment that it and Aquinas's *analogia entis* (appropriately understood) and the *analogia relationis* are not as far apart as they may seem. McCormack has argued that whereas the first is a static given, the latter is dynamic—it is *always being given*. Reflecting the thought of Karl Barth, he states, "The 'analogy of faith' refers most fundamentally to a relation of correspondence between an *act* of God and an *act* of a human subject; the act of divine Self-revelation and the human act of faith in which that revelation is acknowledged. More specifically, the analogy which is established in a revelation event is an analogy between God's knowledge of himself and human knowledge of him in and through human concepts and words."[4] Thus, Christ as the *Logos* of God, veiled in humanity, becomes the sole paradigm for our knowledge, experience, and speech about God. However, in humble submission to the inherent rationality of that self-disclosure, we are able to think God's thoughts after him.

The givenness of the image of God, and our dynamic discovery of ourselves as persons-in-relation, is a fearsome gift—"fearsome" because the loss of persons with whom we are ensconced leads to great pain, "gift" because the capacities we enjoy in relationship are rich, and when we lose our

---

2. Ibid., 13–14.

3. Witvliet, "Doctrine of the Trinity," 263. The complexities of participation have been described elsewhere and cannot be entered into in detail here. Discussions of the merits of material (*methexis*) and relational (*koinōnia*) participation may be found in Hastings, *Life of God in Jonathan Edwards*. My preference for relational participation between persons, human and divine, is reflected throughout this book.

4. McCormack, *Karl Barth's Critically Realistic Dialectical Theology*, 17.

loved ones, the care and comfort of the Divine Persons are there to embrace us and to share in our sorrow.

This aspect of our interpersonal nature, our being in God's being, brings comfort when death comes; in a real sense, death does not destroy the relationship between God and the dying person. It also becomes a source of comfort for those who remain behind, those who undergo the losses and the grief. The wonder of the Christian gospel is that God does not merely forgive and justify people, but does so by bringing them into union with himself. His purposes are filial before they are forensic. Christians are "Christ's ones" because they are "in Christ" and he is in them. This happens because in human history, the Son became one with us by his incarnation, and then, at the conversion point in our soul history, the Holy Spirit made that union real by coming to indwell us. Because the Spirit indwells us, and because he is an interpersonal Person, Christ also lives in us. We are in Christ, and Christ is in us. This is utterly staggering. As Jon Tal Murphree says it, "To be created for personality overlap with God, defies comprehension."[5]

We become one with God, and at home in him, in a relational sense. Jesus said it in these comforting words in John 14:20–23: *"On that day you will realize that I am in my Father, and you are in me, and I am in you. Whoever has my commands and keeps them is the one who loves me. The one who loves me will be loved by my Father, and I too will love them and show myself to them. . . . Anyone who loves me will obey my teaching. My Father will love them, and we will come to them and make our home with them."*

The loss of a home when a spouse dies is one of the most painful aspects of loss. The home can never be the same again. But because we are in Christ by the Spirit, we are always in the ultimate home, the home that all human homes merely point to as a kind of sacrament. By the indwelling of the Spirit, the Father and the Son have already made their home in the heart of every believer. The believer is ensconced in the very heart of the Triune God and embraced by the God of all comfort, who is the Father of compassion, who is the Son who is *"touched with the feeling of our infirmities,"* and who is the Holy Spirit, the come-alongside Comforter. Without minimizing the loss of our earthly homes when losses come—the glaringly empty side of the bed, the reduced circle at the dinner table, the silenced laugh, the absent emotional center, the lost confidant—the road to healing is to find security and comfort in the presence of the eternal Father. The

5. Murphree, *Trinity and Human Personality,* 48.

description Paul uses for a departed Christian is "at home with the Lord." This is a source of hope and comfort for those who are left, to be sure. What makes that hope more real to our present experience is our own spiritual access into that home. It is within individual persons by the immediacy of the presence of the Spirit, and it is among us as the gathered people of God.

There are statistics to suggest that people of faith do better on average with loss and grieving.[6] This is no triumphalistic statistic, however, to be bandied about like a banner of superiority, or to be used to bash Christians who don't do well, nor to short-circuit the genuine grieving process.

All Humanity?

What does this mean for humanity in general? What if a person is not a Christian? Can they be well individuated and mutually relational persons in community? Can they also experience the comfort of God in grief?

Humans did not cease to bear the image of God when they sinned at the beginning of human history. Genesis 9, written well after the fall, speaks of the sacredness of human life because humans are made in the image of God. We are still God-like creatures, capable of amazing accomplishments in our use of creation's resources given to us to steward as image-bearers of God, but also capable of shocking destructiveness related to our self-orientation and the sinful impulses that pervade the human soul. Instead of God-oriented selves, persons curved towards God, sinful selves become turned in on themselves (*in curvatus in se*). People manage their lives and their God-given resources independently, in ways that violate the nature of their interpersonal selves. The nature of humans as image bearers has always been a gift granted by God, not so much a *given* as *something given* in sheer grace. Whether Christian or not, humans are formally in the image of God. They have horizontal capacities with other humans, such as to be individuated and yet live in healthy relationships. They are in relatedness to God, as recipients of their life and breath and being. However, a spiritual disconnect in all human beings prevents them from being in relationship (not merely relatedness) with God.

Let me illustrate. I am related to quite a few cousins in the UK, but for practical reasons, I do not know them all. I have a relationship with some who have visited us frequently over the years. I have a relatedness to others, but am not actively in relationship with them.

6. See Sullender, *Grief and Growth*, chapter 8.

What does being in relationship (and not merely relatedness) to the Triune God bring to human persons? By sheer grace—and not because they are better than anyone else, or have greater natural capacities or a healthier relational background or psychological health (often the opposite is true)—people who have been regenerated and reconciled to God through Christ's person and work are in actual living *union* with the Triune God. They are given resources for the restoration of their brokenness and for recovery towards the fullness of the image of God. Being in union with Christ (the NT describes this in its most crucial prepositional phrase as "in Christ"), they are freed by justification from the burden of guilt; and being in union with Christ in death and resurrection, they are launched into a process of spiritual and emotional transformation to become more fully who they were created to be—as persons, in a richer mutuality of communion with God and other humans, including their significant others. Through the resources of the Holy Spirit who actually indwells the Christian, and who makes Christ present in the communion of the church, the Christian person can know healing and the recovery of what it means to be a human person-in-relation, fully alive.

This process of transformation must not be construed as simple, quick, or easy. It is a journey in which transformation is opposed by demonic forces, indwelling sin, intransigent defense mechanisms, and cultural seductions. In the process we are active, not passive. God's agency and our agency are compatibilist rather than synergistic. In other words, just because divine action is needed to bring humans back to spiritual life in order to reflect the material, rather than the merely formal imaging of God, human action is real and necessary. In other words, divine initiative and action do not destroy the integrity of human action. They actually free our action to be precisely human in the best sense of that term. This frees the human person to once again be the *interpersonal* person that an image-bearing person by definition *is*.

Personal and communal spiritual practices are involved that require discipline, even if the discipline is simply providing space for relationship with God, instead of self-motivated grit. Living life in the sacred rhythms of grace is required for the Christian person's healing and sanctification, and sadly, this is the "road less traveled" for many reasons. In our time, many persons of other religions, and often purely secular people, reflect more character and image-bearing qualities than professed Christians who have never moved much beyond their profession of faith.

The comfort of God in the midst of loss is extended to all people. God is *for* the world. His face shines on even the most image-marred human being. He seeks the lost, especially when they hit rock bottom. He seeks them all the way to the point of death. It is true that being in relationship with God gives access to the comfort of the "God of all comfort," but God's intention is to woo and redeem and reconcile every human life. In caring for dying or bereaved people, I believe it is safe to assume God is at work in their hearts, and that as we walk in the Spirit, we are participating in what God may be up to in them, even as they grapple with what is happening.

The church has often viewed itself as a *bounded* set, with a solid line between the church and the world. It is true that the people of God are to be distinctive, holy, other—in the sense that they march to the beat of a different drum, a kingdom drum. This is a separation from the world as ideological. But as far as the *people* of the world are concerned, I believe it is better for the church to see itself a *centered* set, devoted to deep worship, teaching, discipleship, and fellowship, yet always with an openness to and *active* hospitality towards all of humanity, and especially those in crisis, in loss, in death. People need to know they belong before they believe. The church's opportunity to minister to dying and grieving people by presence and caring is vast. This is often a time of great spiritual openness. I have found this true every time I am invited as a pastor to take a memorial service for people with no prior connection to the church. I have also experienced in palpable ways what it means to be participating with the Triune God in his work in the families of these people.

Much more will be said in later chapters about God's participation in our suffering, our experience of that union with Christ in the midst of suffering, and how caregivers (whether friends, counselors, or pastors) can participate with God as a *koinōnia* on behalf of the great divine *Koinōnia* in his comforting, healing, and transformative ministry to the dying and grieving. When humans model the Trinity as persons-in-relation by means of their participation in Christ, they give ample evidence of the theo-anthropological conviction that human persons have an interpersonal self. This in turn gives insight into the nature and gravity of grief.

We now turn our attention to the confirmation of this way of seeing human beings in contemporary human psychology.

chapter 7

The Source and Nature of Grief

INSIGHTS FROM PSYCHOLOGY

I AM FASCINATED BY psychological accounts of grief and grieving that are based on the presupposition that people are interpersonal, and that when they lose significant relationships, "a part of the self is experienced as lost." One school of thought suggests that grief be considered as *separation anxiety*. In this sense, grief is understood as "an acute fear in the self over the loss or threat to lose a segment of the self associated with the lost object."[1] Psychologists of this school relate this to the primal separation anxiety we all experience when we leave our mother's womb. John Bowlby, operating on the basis of an ethological rather than psychoanalytic model, affirms that "separation anxiety in the human infant is the prototype of all adult grief."[2] David Switzer, a pastoral theologian influenced by the psychoanalytic tradition of Harry Stack Sullivan, has noted through experience that an acute grief reaction bears strong similarity to a classic anxiety attack in terms of the accompanying symptoms, as well as the defense mechanisms that the self utilizes to lessen the severity of the pain and anxiety.

One symptom of grief that makes sense of the "separation anxiety" understanding is regressive or childish behavior. The primal childhood fear of abandonment is relived. When adults are bereaved they "cry like a baby," and they develop strong dependency behaviors that would not be normal for them, such as "holding on" and becoming unusually clingy.

---

1. Sullender, *Grief and Growth*, 28.
2. Bowlby, *Attachment and Loss, Vol. 2*, 16.

I was not conscious of this clinginess in me until a new relationship developed, two-and-a-half years after losing Sharon. My own experience of it was, in retrospect, rather embarrassing. The slightest delay in the return of a text message led to anxiety out of all proportion to the situation. I suspect that at a deep level, I was afraid to lose another person I loved. I suspect that this insecurity and dependency was also fed from a deeper place in me, the early abandonment experience I have already described.[3] If Bowlby and others are right, it also tapped into the loss I experienced when I left the womb!

Are there antidotes for these symptoms? At the right time, when grief processing is sufficiently well along, a new love relationship may be the best cure. However, the new spouse may need to be particularly understanding of the high dependency needs a bereaved person may have in the initial stages of a new relationship. Though this clinginess may be slightly irritating for support people, they nevertheless need to show extra grace and understanding, and to bond as closely as they can. This does not mean they may not have to occasionally speak frankly to the grieving person, to draw them out of obsessiveness and possessiveness. The pressure can be taken off the supporting spouse if the grieving person also is part of a close, supportive community of friends and family. For as Sullender suggests, "the best antidote to separation anxiety is people."[4] In all cases, helping the bereaved person to "talk it out" is important for their healing. More severe cases may require talking it out with a professional grief counselor or therapist, who can be thought of as a specially gifted person in community with the griever, with appropriate skills and boundaries.

Defense mechanisms, including denial, repression, idealization, and identification, are utilized when pain or reality is too great to bear. They are in one sense a gift from God, necessary for our protection until our psyches can process our loss. But when used too severely or "employed too rigidly or for too long a time" they "can actually block the healing process."[5]

In some ways, this seems to describe the shock reaction when death occurs. I can remember being warned in the days leading up to Sharon's

---

3. Lifelong research by John Bowlby and others has shown considerable evidence that disruptions of bonding between mothers and children between the ages of six months and six years old are causally related to insecurity, depression, and disturbed personality development. See Bowlby, *Making and Breaking of Affectional Bonds*, 45.

4. Sullender, *Grief and Growth*, 30.

5. I am relying here on the summary of Switzer's work offered in Sullender, *Grief and Growth*, 27–28.

departure, "Now, you are going to be in shock when she dies." Sharon had been battling ovarian cancer for twenty-one months, and she had been in palliative care for close to three weeks. I was tempted to think I might have gotten my mind ready for the moment of her death. But I would have been so wrong. It is a shock, no matter how long the suffering has gone on, no matter how sudden or "expected" the death may be. Death is *not* normal to our human experience or life cycle, no matter how much we may try cerebrally to believe that. It may have been part of "normal existence" for animals in the eons before humanity received its coronation as bearers of the image of God, but for the first image bearers, spiritual death came as a result of the fall. God's intent for them was perpetuity of existence, eternal life in union with him, experiencing his presence with them on earth as they managed it for him. Paul certainly spoke of death as the "*last enemy to be destroyed*" (1 Cor 15:26) by the death and resurrection of Jesus. Yes, it will be swallowed up in the victory that Christ, the last Adam (the first intended Adam, the *eschatos* Adam) has accomplished by his resurrection. But this will not be finally enacted until his second coming. In the meantime, this era when the kingdom has come but not yet fully, we still struggle with death. It still shocks us.

Yet another way of seeing grief that is underpinned by an interpersonal view of the human person is grief *as a process of realization*. This is consonant with our thought that grief is shock-thaw, the fresh expression of feelings as we slowly thaw out from shock and come to terms with the full impact of our loss.

Consonance in the Field of Psychological Science on the Interpersonal Self

Another way to say this is that we are built to love. Just as the Trinity is defined as Love, we are created to be loved and to love one another. Love is the foundation of human existence. Unfortunately this means that in a fallen world, love is costly and grief is inevitable. Because of sin, interpersonal selves can deeply hurt one another. And persons defined by relations can, in a fallen world in which death exists, be deeply affected by wrenching loss. "A part of me has died," many say. According to the interpersonal-self viewpoint, this is actually true.

The idea of an interpersonal self has been advocated in the field of psychology by people such as Ronald Fairbairn. Whereas Freud identified people in a subject's environment with the term "object"—e.g., to identify a person as the "object" of a drive, so that infants developed around these drives—Fairbairn posited that human infants were not seeking the satisfaction of drives, but rather actually seeking the satisfaction that comes in relation to real others. From birth, and even before it, we are formed by the other.

In the psychoanalytic tradition, Harry Stack Sullivan[6] also proposed the idea of an interpersonal self, and pastoral theologian David Switzer built on this. Switzer describes the development of the self in a growing child as she interrelates with her family and environment. He offered the opinion that speech/language was the mechanism of the interaction, speech being the means of interacting with others but at the same time the means of identifying and clarifying who she is. He expresses the interpersonal nature of the self in this way: "The foundation of the Self is comprised of the internalized response of the significant other. The individual self is interpersonal at its core, arising out of and continuing to be dependent upon the other."[7]

This leads Switzer, among many others in the psychoanalytic tradition,[8] to conclude that grief is actually separation anxiety. Roos and Neimeyer emphasize the once-for-all nature of the moment of loss, either when a diagnosis is given or when actual death occurs, as "the trauma that marks the moment of one's expulsion from a metaphorical Eden."[9] John Bowlby, of the ethological rather than psychoanalytic school, articulates also the interpersonal nature of the self and expresses the same sentiment concerning grief. He speaks of the separation anxiety in the human infant as the "prototype of all adult grief."[10] The fear associated with death is fear of the loss of the self through separation. I suggest that it accounts also for the shock factor in death.

---

6. See Sullivan, *The Interpersonal Theory of Psychiatry* and *The Collected Works of Harry Stack Sullivan, Vol. 1 and 2.* Though Freud's ideas about instinct, drives, and complexes (oedipal, etc.) are by no means mainstream today, he did leave the lasting legacy of an understanding of the "intrapsychic" dynamics of the mind, which in turn was a starting point for some of his followers to move on to interpersonal understandings of the human person (e.g., Heinz Kohut and Sullivan).

7. Switzer, *Dynamics of Grief,* 83.

8. Sullender comments that "The centrality and importance of separation anxiety in grief is now widely accepted by scholars and writers." Sullender, *Grief and Growth,* 28.

9. Roos and Neimeyer, "Reauthoring the Self," 94.

10. Bowlby, *Attachment and Loss, Vol. 2,* 16.

How a person accommodates the loss of a loved one also accords with the notion of the "interpersonal self." Jacques Derrida refers to the fact that "even the proper name seems to refer, in the wake of death, not to the deceased but only to him or her in us, in memory."[11] Thus, Derrida states, "When I say Roland Barthes it is certainly him whom I name, him beyond his name. But since he himself is now inaccessible to this appellation, since this nomination cannot become a vocation, address, or apostrophe, . . . it is him in me that I name, toward him in me, in you, in us that I pass through his name."[12] Tammy Clewell summarizes Derrida's understanding of mourning "as an affirmative incorporation of the lost other, emphasizing that we internalize lost loves [while] at the same time the lost other cannot be fully assimilated in the mourner's psyche." While recognizing that otherness in the self may give rise to forms of melancholy depression, Derrida also argues that the mourning subject "welcomes" its own bereaved decentering as the very condition of "hospitality, love or friendship."[13]

There is something to be learned from how a number of psychological schools of thought (humanistic, psychoanalytic, cognitive behavioral, attachment theory) have viewed grief. The theme of the interpersonal self recurs in some of these traditions. We now visit three of these very briefly.

Psychoanalytic Theory

In trying to understand the nature of grief, we may consider first the psychoanalytic approach grounded largely on the work of Sigmund Freud. This involves probing not just the conscious but the unconscious thought and motivation of human behavior. It puts great emphasis also on various instincts and fantasies that Freud viewed to be defense mechanisms against pain. The common affects that characterize mourning and melancholia were what attracted Freud's attention.[14] It seems, however, that he was much more interested in what mourning revealed about depression than the other way around.[15] In fact, Martine Lussier suggests in her evaluation of

11. Derrida, *Work of Mourning*, trans. Brault and Naas, editors' introduction, 10.

12. Ibid., 46.

13. Clewell, "Mourning Beyond Melancholia" (the Derrida quotations are from *Work of Mourning*), 188.

14. See Freud, "Mourning and Melancholia," 239–60.

15. Freud's work on depression is still highly valued by the psychiatric profession, as evidenced by the work of a group of researchers who in 2008 published that their

Freud's understanding of bereavement that he was "relatively uninterested in the normal model of mourning, especially when compared with all that flowed from his work on dreams."[16] Interestingly, in the context of his own father's death, Freud speaks of the death of a father as "the most important event, the most poignant loss of a man's life."[17] Lussier asks, wouldn't the death of the mother be more important? Then in agreement with Freud she explains that the loss of a father "simultaneously activates both the incestuous fantasy and the parricidal fantasy."[18]

Not all in the field of psychological research agree on what Freud said with respect to grief and "recovery"—or, as is the preferred term, "adaptation"[19]—following it. Ruth Konigsberg, in a popular article on grief in *TIME* magazine,[20] seeks to debunk various popularly held myths about grief and attributes the "myth" of the "grief work hypothesis" to Freud. By this, she means the definition of grief "as a project that must be tackled in order to prevent psychological problems." "This notion," she states, "can be traced back to Freud, who wrote that the 'work of mourning' was for the ego to detach itself from the deceased so that it could reattach itself to someone else." This metaphor, she insists, became "the guiding metaphor for modern grief theory" in the 1970s. She goes on to cite "the 60-person study conducted by the husband-and-wife research team Wolfgang and Margaret Stroebe of Utrecht University" who "found that widows who avoided confronting their loss were not any more depressed than widows who 'worked through' their grief." She also points to the work of the Stroebes, who demonstrated in several studies that "talking or writing about the death of a spouse did not help people adjust to that loss any better."[21]

---

empirical findings in neuropsychiatry were consonant with the principles Freud had proposed in his metapsychology. See Carhart-Harris et al., "Mourning and Melancholia Revisited."

16. Lussier, "Mourning and Melancholia," 667. This article is helpful in examining the foundations on which Freud based his conception of mourning, both internal (his own grief experiences) and external (the scholarly influences that shaped his thought).

17. Freud, *The Interpretation of Dreams* (1900), xxvi, cited in Lussier, "Mourning and Melancholia," 668.

18. Lussier, "Mourning and Melancholia," 668.

19. Worden, *Grief Counseling*, xiv.

20. Ruth Davis Konigsberg, "New Ways to Think about Grief," *TIME*, January 29, 2011, 1–4. http://content.time.com/time/magazine/article/0,9171,2042372–1,00.html. This article is adapted from her book, *The Truth About Grief: The Myth of Its Five Stages and the New Science of Loss* (New York: Simon & Schuster, 2011).

21. Ruth Davis Konigsberg, "New Ways to Think about Grief," 2. See also M. S.

Similarly, Worden cites Freud in "Mourning and Melancholia" as seeing grieving as a natural process that "should not be tampered with," which he interprets to mean that Freud did not think acute grief needed to be managed.[22]

Though Freudian insights have their place, and many approaches that have come since Freud owe much to him, I find that more relational approaches to psychology, such as object relations theory (Fairbairn) and attachment theory (Bowlby), are more helpful in general and especially with respect to understanding grief.

Object Relations Theory

Daniel Price has demonstrated an interesting link between Karl Barth's analogy of relations and the *object relations theory* of human development developed by Scottish psychologist R. D. W. Fairbairn.[23] Fairbairn challenges Freud's individualistic determinism, with respect to the psychological understanding of humanity, with the determinative impact of key human interactions with others in the development of the person.[24] The assumption of the analogy (by model and participation) between the three persons of the Trinity and humans in relationship is, of course, that human persons are deeply interdependent and yet secure in their own identity. Therefore, healthy personal encounters and relationships should not lead to loss of identity, but rather to its strengthening. Loss of a loved one should therefore leave the core identity of the mourner intact. For both metaphysical and moral reasons, this is never achieved in human life on this side of the new creation. When a person loses another with whom they have become one

---

Stroebe, R. O. Hansson, H. Schut, and W. Stroebe (eds.), *Handbook of Bereavement Research and Practice.*

22. Worden, *Grief Counseling,* 83.

23. See Price, *Karl Barth's Anthropology.*

24. Ibid., See also Price, "Issues Related to Human Nature," 170–80. Price comments: "In object relations self-identity develops only within the history of complex social interaction. The child is born within a social matrix, and the self develops likewise. For Barth, of course, the social coefficient of knowing and being has a theological foundation. From Barth's theological perspective the social matrix of human personhood reflects the relational character of the Triune God. God is a being who is in relation to himself: not just within the economic Trinity, but also within the immanent Trinity. In other words: God does not pretend to be triune, nor become triune, merely to save us—he actually is a triune community eternally. This is one of the basic tenets of Nicene orthodoxy."

in every sense, grief is inevitable. The self that has been healthily formed by the other (the one who has died) has been lost, as well as any dependencies that were unhealthy. It seems to me that distinguishing these is important in the grief process. Derrida's description of the loss of a person, by means of the hospitality to that person within one's own personhood, is compatible with this tradition.

Attachment Theory

The development of *attachment theory* by British psychoanalyst John Bowlby (1907–90) has been described in detail elsewhere.[25] This is a short summary of his research and conclusions. Bowlby's observation of the behaviors of young children who were separated from their parents and placed in institutions led him to delineate three phases: protest, despair, and detachment. During the first phase, the children showed significant separation distress, such as crying, screaming, and searching for the missing family member, often the mother. The second phase was characterized by loss of hope of the return of the parent, and the children becoming increasingly withdrawn. In the last phase, that of detachment, the children became open to adult caregivers and peers, and when reintroduced to their parents, their demeanor did not demonstrate joy, but rather, apathy. Some of these children turned away from their mothers and resisted reconnection. Bowlby's work, seeking to understand the causes and purposes of these behaviors that followed separation, led to his publishing the three-volume *Attachment and Loss* (1969, 1973, 1980),[26] which is the bible of attachment theory.

A brief summary description of the work of Bowlby is as follows:[27]

- The behaviors of the children when separated from their families were called "attachment behaviors."

- These behaviors were intended to foster physical proximity to the caregiver, also termed the "attachment figure," often the mother.

---

25. See Kelley, *Grief,* 54–59, for a good but short summary of the theory and its chief proponents and those who have integrated it with Christian theology. See also Sue Johnson, *Hold Me Tight,* for a good summation of attachment theory and its impact on marriage and relationships.

26. See bibliography for full citations. See also Bowlby, *Making and Breaking of Affectional Bonds.*

27. I follow here the summary description in Kelley, *Grief,* 55–56.

- "Consistent physical *proximity* to the caregiver" and her "appropriate *responsiveness* to the needs of the infant" facilitate a "secure attachment" in the infant, which plays "a substantial role in one's capacity to form secure relationships in later life."

- By contrast, a child "who forms insecure attachments in infancy may also struggle with insecure relationships later in life."

- Bowlby maintained that "attachment behavior is an instinctual and constitutive dimension of being human and endures throughout the lifespan," a claim supported empirically by the work of Kaplan, Sadock, and Grebb.[28]

- Bowlby's colleague Mary Ainsworth, based on laboratory observations of mothers and infants, proposed three slightly differently nuanced patterns or styles of infant response to separation: "secure," "avoidant," and "resistant/ambivalent."[29]

- "Infants with a secure style of attachment have come, through experience, to expect their caregivers to be both accessible and responsive to their needs, and they thus feel more confident to explore and engage with the world."

- Infants "with insecure attachments do not have the same confidence in the accessibility of their caregivers" given that they have not found their caregivers to be consistently available, and that "attachment behaviors are sometimes ignored or even rebuffed."

- Of these insecurely attached infants, some may be designated as "anxious-ambivalent" (analogous to Ainsworth's "resistant/ambivalent") or as "avoidant."

- "Infants with an *anxious-ambivalent* attachment style fear rejection by their attachment figures and become preoccupied with eliciting comfort and security from them . . . their attachment system tends to be chronically activated."

- Infants with "an *avoidant* attachment style have also come to anticipate rejection or lack of responsiveness . . . and to suppress attachment feelings and behaviors as a defense against rejection. . . . As children and adults, they may demonstrate what Bowlby describes as "compulsive

28. See Kaplan et al., *Kaplan and Sadock's Synopsis of Psychiatry.*
29. See Ainsworth et al., *Patterns of Attachment.*

self-reliance . . . maintaining emotional distance and limiting intimacy as a defensive, self-protective strategy."

- In collaboration with Ainsworth, Bowlby refined his theory regarding the goal of attachment behaviors and the effects of separation. It was proposed in Bowlby's second volume that security in attachment derives from a child's appraisal of an attachment figure as available and accessible, and as responsive (defined as willingness to comfort and protect). Bowlby then proposed the term *availability* as inclusive of both the accessibility and the responsiveness of the caregiver, which could then be used as "the goal of the attachment behavioral system."

- The expectations that one has of attachment figure availability "are functions of internal working models, which are 'cognitive/affective schemas, or representations' (Bartholomew & Shaver, 1998, 25[30]) of both self and others that are formed as a result of one's actual experience in attachment relationships."

- Our internal working models may become more complex as we grow older, but they are not in constant flux, tending to "remain fairly stable in terms of the attachment relationship (secure or insecure) they reflect and are somewhat resistant to change."

- One measure of security is that of tendency towards exploration. Ainswort comments that infants tend to turn to an attachment figure as a "secure base from which to explore"[31] the environment. Bowlby built on the concept of the "secure base," to express a central principle in his concept of parenting.

This brings me to a central feature of my concept of parenting: the provision by both parents of a secure base from which a child or an adolescent can make sorties into the outside world, and to which he can return knowing that he will be welcomed, nourished physically and emotionally, comforted if distressed, and reassured if frightened. In essence, this role is one of being available, ready to respond when called upon to encourage and perhaps assist, but to intervene actively only when clearly necessary. We see children and adolescents, as they get older, venturing steadily farther from the base and for increasing spans of time. The more confident they are that their base is secure, and ready if called upon to respond, the more they take it for granted. Yet should one or other parent become ill or

30. Bartholomew and Shaver, "Methods of Assessing Adult Attachment," 25.

31. Ainsworth et al., *Patterns of Attachment*, 265.

die, the immense significance of the base to the emotional equilibrium of the child or adolescent or young adult is at once apparent.[32]

This leads us to express the nature of grief as a "deep sense of disequilibrium," for if it entails the loss of the attachment figures of our life, we are left without that secure base. Kelley quotes the well-known saying of C. S. Lewis, on the loss of his much-loved wife Joy, "No one ever told me that grief felt so like fear." She then states,

> From an attachment perspective, the linkage of grief and fear makes perfect sense. Separation from one's attachment figure can trigger great anxiety, and the permanent loss of this figure can shake one at the most basic level, leaving one scared and adrift for a time. For someone with an insecure style of attachment, the loss may take an even greater toll, confirming one's expectations that life offers little safety and security.[33]

This idea of a secure base from which to explore reminds me of the sentiments of Psalm 131. The psalmist says, "But I have calmed and quieted myself, I am like a weaned child with its mother; like a weaned child I am content." The first part of the psalm expresses the humility of the person who moves out in discovery, but knows that there are limits and is therefore not arrogant about the pursuit of knowledge. This second verse, however, points to the security and contentment of a godly and secure soul. The psalmist's soul is like a weaned child with his mother. The image here is not of an infant, but of a slightly older child. The process of weaning may have been painful, but once weaned, this child shows the inner security and contentment of having an attachment figure who is there and responsive when needed. This child knows he will still be fed, but he has been given the freedom and individuation needed to explore. The psalmist is using this analogy, however, to speak of the soul of a mature person whose attachment figure is God. The idea of attachment to God is explored in Melissa Kelley's book *Grief*, in which she has outlined ways of extending pastoral care to bereaved people based on this concept of God as the ultimate attachment figure of the human soul. We will consider this concept in a later chapter.

One real-life person with a secure attachment, in my judgment, is Bill Hybels, the famed Chicago pastor. In his premarital counseling book written with his wife Lynne, *Fit to Be Tied*, he recounts how at age fourteen he was allowed to steer his father's two-million-dollar yacht when his father

32. Bowlby, *A Secure Base: Parent-Child Attachment*, 11.

33. Kelley, *Grief*, 58–59.

handed him the controls and went to sleep. This was an adolescent given a secure base from which to explore! There came a time when Bill lost his father. I remember hearing that he went through a disequilibrating season of grief and ultimately found, in his Father God, a sense of shalom again.

Consonance in the Field of Psychological Science on the Shock-Thaw Factor

All the schools of psychological thought express, in one form or another, the shock that occurs when loved ones are lost, the slowness with which shock dissipates, and the importance of realism with respect to full resolution of the loss. By way of example, Susan Roos[34] writes about the journey of loss experienced by psychologist Paul Barber[35] upon the diagnosis and progression of disease of his partner, Anna. Roos touchingly notes that "She was his most shining attribute, and his identity was interwoven with hers." Anna had been diagnosed with Alzheimer's dementia. This kind of loss is sometimes referred to as "ambiguous loss" (it is also "double loss"—that in diagnosis, and that when death comes), but the same principles apply to other losses also. Roos writes that "Barber describes his first realization of his partner's dementia as his world being torn apart and as self-deconstruction. This was his existential wake-up call. He was exquisitely aware that he would never again be the same. In my professional experience, the awareness of oneself and one's life as forever changed is often slow in coming; not so with Barber." Despite acknowledging this quick awareness of shock in Barber, Roos notes the "trauma associated with his loss," and speaks of the hard work in Gestalt therapy that enabled him, "rather than being dissociated . . . to lean into the pain, a Gestalt process of focusing-in and meeting what is." She summarizes his experience as one of "narrative disruption, as expressed in his journaling," which "is exemplary of a determination not to fall prey to narrative dissociation; i.e., stories of loss that are unvoiced to others—and not even to the self . . . ."[36]

However, even in this instance Roos is frank about the reality that closure is slow and never complete. She does speak of partial closure: "From a field perspective, in such cases there are often pressures for 'closure,' i.e. for relinquishing bonds with the person who is lost (Melnick and Roos, 2007),

34. See Roos, "Chronic Sorrow and Ambiguous Loss."
35. See Barber, *Becoming a Practitioner Researcher*.
36. Roos, "Chronic Sorrow and Ambiguous Loss," 230–31.

even in a person whose loss is ambiguous. It is possible that fragmentary closure and closure for many aspects of the loss may occur periodically as consequences of new understandings, shifts in perspective, philosophical growth, and new life experiences and attributions of meaning."[37] However, adding a touch of realism, Roos notes the long-term nature of the struggle: "The task of re-learning the self and the world is usually arduous and often overwhelming. It may be the beneficial focus of attention and concern for all the remaining years of our lives. Closure for the loss (traditionally defined as completion, decathexis, or resolution) is rarely valid or feasible. Moreover, many benefits, most unforeseen, often accompany the sorrow that is the result of significantly life-changing loss." She adds that "in keeping with Gestalt theory . . . avoidance of dissociation and isolation/compartmentalization of the loss is possible and beneficial in the sense that life is enlarged, enriched, and more soulful."[38]

While maintaining that complete closure is "myth," Roos does describe some reasonable expectations of a grieving journey:

> Restoration of resilience can take place when one knows fully and intimately what has been lost, and when regulatory reactions such as crying and pain can have their day without censorship or repression. Other benefits may consist of bearing witness, holding memories, healing and/or reconfiguring a conflicted relationship with the one who is lost, integrating new understandings of the self in relation to the loss, channeling energy resulting from the tension of non-closure into positive, life-affirming pursuits, developing greater compassion and empathic accuracy, and finding life more deeply appreciated in the context of suffering (Melnick and Roos, 2007).[39]

Implicit in an understanding of the difficulty in resolving grief towards closure is the possibility that there can be "complicated grief," often manifesting with similar symptoms such as depression. The question as to whether complicated grief should be a category with the DSM-V is controversial.[40] "Camouflaged grief" is also a possibility when the shock-thawing

37. Ibid., 230.

38. Ibid.

39. Ibid. The article referred to is Melnick and Roos, "The Myth of Closure." *Gestalt Review* 11.2 (2007) 90–107.

40. See Larson, "Taking Stock." This is a review of *Beyond Kübler-Ross: New Perspectives on Death, Dying and Grief*, edited by Kenneth J. Doka and Amy S. Tucci. Washington, DC: Hospice Foundation of America, 2011.

process is circumvented in various ways, or the trauma caused by grief goes underground. Dale Larson, in his review of grief therapy, makes reference to this kind of grief:

> My own view concerning the grief work hypothesis is that emotional processing, positive affect, and even denial can all play important roles in healthy self-regulation and we must avoid exalting one at the expense of the others (Larson & Hoyt, 2007). As someone conducting research on self-concealment, I find Balk's discussions of adolescents camouflaging their grief, and bereaved parents' reluctance to acknowledge the continuing bonds they maintained with their dead child, quite fascinating.[41]

These complicated and camouflaged griefs are a consequence of underestimating the interpersonal nature of the human self, and that of the departed loved ones.

---

41. Larson, "Taking Stock," 350. The articles cited are: D. G. Larson and T. W. Hoyt, "The Bright Side of Grief Counseling: Deconstructing the New Pessimism," in Doka (ed.), *Living with Grief,* 157–74; and Balk, "Grief Counseling without the Grief," 346–48.

chapter 8

Moving towards Adaptation—

GRIEF SHARING WITH THE TRIUNE GOD
IN DECONSTRUCTION

I am inclined to contend—along the lines of Eugene Peterson's take on Eliot's "teach us to care and not to care"—that optimal care cannot be provided without a "first-order relationship." Without some grounding in deep meaning, intent to care may be well-intentioned, but almost invariably goes astray.

—*Dr James Holmlund, psychiatrist*[1]

Grief Shared with God (Attachment to God)

CRUCIAL TO THIS BOOK, then, is the reality of grief-sharing between God and the bereaved. In the midst of suffering and grief, the Triune God, who has entered into the pain of the world in Christ, draws us into his inner life and love. He shares it. He carries it. He comforts us. He redeems it in ways that are both seen and unseen in this life. He transforms us even, and especially, in our most vulnerable and broken seasons. He is intimately present to us in the present. He offers ultimate hope of a resurrection day in the future. A new creation.

Of course, timing for such theological talk is everything. For those who try to circumvent the grief process, their own or that of others, by using a theology of hope as a denial mechanism for avoiding their feelings of loss, Richard Neuhaus has the following words: "For those sitting on the

1. By way of an e-mail to me on August 13, 2014.

81

mourning bench of the eternal pity, however, that triumphant note will ring hollow."[2]

A classic case of this happened about three months after Sharon died. A well-intentioned gentleman from my own congregation asked after church how I was doing, expecting the pat answer we often give, "Just great, thanks!" I expressed that I was journeying well and that I had good days and bad. His quick response was, "You will see her again, you know!" I confess to experiencing more than a little anger, the force of which, fortunately, I did not express in the moment! Often, people say these kinds of things because they are just uncomfortable. They don't know what to say. But a better response might have been, "I haven't been through such a loss, and can only imagine the pain. I am praying for you."

This is also the problem with upbeat funeral services that are a celebration of life without giving space for grief (because it's "embarrassing"). They short-circuit "the *Dies Irae* of sin, loss, and judgment." Neuhaus says that

> A good many Christians . . . have imbibed too well Platonic notions of an immortal soul floating off to paradise or even Buddhist ideas of the unreality of death, and therefore the unreality of life as well. The attitude seems to be, "Death? It's no big deal." But for those dying their own death and the death of those they love, death is a very big deal indeed. Don't tell them that it doesn't matter, that they'll get over it, that things will look brighter tomorrow. Death is, in the words of St. Paul, "the last enemy" (1 Cor 15:26). *The only consolation to be trusted is the consolation that is on the far side of the inconsolable.*[3]

Thus, I don't, on the one hand, wish to minimize the mystery of death and grief by being either simplistic or triumphalistic. While the work of Elizabeth Kubler-Ross, defining five stages of grief, may be helpful for giving permission for mourners to experience what they do in grieving, it can be used reductionistically (e.g., some people "apparently know where they

---

2. Neuhaus, *Eternal Pity*, 22.

3. Ibid., emphasis mine. Similarly, Scott Sullender warns of the danger of denial, in response to Melissa Kelley's section on attachment to God as compensation for loss of attachment when a loved one dies. See Sullender, "Grief's Multi-dimensional Nature." Specifically he states, "While helpful, there is a danger in this approach. The efforts of unsophisticated ministers to help mourners to get close to God in a time of loss may function as a form of denial or avoidance of the raw human emotions of grief" (ibid., 114).

are in their trek"[4]). A better approach is rather to encourage reticence in the midst of mystery and to be present to death and to grief, "without any felt urgencies about doing something about it or getting over it." Neuhaus adds that the Preacher in Ecclesiastes had it right: "There is a time to mourn and a time to dance"; that is, "the time of mourning should be given its due."[5] He adds, "One may be permitted to wonder at the wisdom of contemporary funeral rites that hurry to the dancing, displacing sorrow with the determined affirmation of resurrection hope, supplying a ready answer to a question that has not been given time to understand itself."[6]

But there does come a time when theology must be affirmed and when the redemptive purpose of grief must be searched out, and when transformation will begin to be noticed as we take a backward glance. I don't mean for a minute that loss and grief should be viewed as punishment (except in some rare cases the Scriptures relate, such as 1 Corinthians 11 and James 5), or that there is ever a simple cause-effect relationship between suffering and transformation. It is much more mysterious than that. But there is a relationship between suffering—including loss and grief—and spiritual growth, a relationship that the Scriptures affirm in both Old and New Testaments. And it is incumbent upon us not to waste the opportunity for growth. As Neuhaus states, "The worst thing is not the sorrow or the loss or the heartbreak. Worse is to be encountered by death and not to be changed by the encounter. There are pills we can take to get through the experience, but the danger is that we do not go through the experience but around it."[7]

When the time comes to speak of theology and spirituality and transformation in grief, I believe the reality of grief-sharing is an all-important motif.

Union with (Attachment to) the Triune God

. . . That Infuses His Sympathy and Comfort
(in Deconstruction, the Acute Phase of Grief)

The notion of grief-sharing is important firstly, and most importantly, because this is what Scripture affirms about suffering in general and grief in

4. Neuhaus, *Eternal Pity*, 3.

5. Ibid.

6. Ibid., 3–4.

7. Ibid., 4.

particular: God enters into it. God, in Christ, by the Holy Spirit, shares in our grief, offering sympathy and thereby beginning the work of the redemption of grief. This redemption comes in stages: God is immediately present to us in all our losses, in our acute grief (an illustration of this is the supportive counseling when a person is acutely depressed). Over the course of time, as his gift of shock thaws out, God works towards sufficient resolution to allow us to function; with the further passing of time, character is formed in us (this is analogous to the more in-depth, probing counseling when a depressed patient is stabilized). And we are enabled to comfort others with the comfort we have received.

Realism is needed, however, in a fallen world into which the kingdom has come, but has not yet fully come. Full resolution of pain and loss and identity-healing awaits resurrection day. But of this we may be assured: In all of the ambiguity and imperfect resolution, God shares our grief. He carries our sorrows. "Surely He took up our pain and bore our suffering," says Isaiah (53:4, NIV). In The Message, it reads, "But the fact is, it was our pain He carried—our disfigurements, all the things wrong with us" (Isa 53:4, Message).

Every believer in Jesus is at home with the Father and the Son, *now*, because the Spirit's indwelling imparts the presence of the Son (by perichoresis, that is the mutual indwelling of each person of the Trinity in the other, such that when one is present, so is the other) and because the Father is in the Son and the Son is in the Father. This is real reality now. We are being drawn ever towards the inner perichoretic life of the Trinity. We are there now, by the Spirit's indwelling, even when we have difficulty experientially entering into that reality. When we are beatified, as our loved ones are now, we will be "at home with the Lord" (2 Cor 5:8), "forever with the Lord" (1 Thess 5:17), which is to say, forever cradled in the inner life of the Trinity. But in my experience, those who lose loved ones are drawn especially close to the Lord in their grieving.

A major theme in the book of Hebrews is the sympathetic ministry of our Great High Priest, Jesus, the Son of God. His becoming human qualified him to feel as humans feel. His endless life now, as a man at the right hand of the Father interceding for us, assures us that he *still* feels and he still *cares*. The writer of Hebrews uses his titles for Christ with care. In 4:14–16, as he expounds Christ's priestly ministry as sympathizer and as one able to impart mercy and grace for the "time of need" (which must include our times of loss), he prefaces the description this way: "Therefore, since we have a great high priest who has ascended into heaven, *Jesus the Son of God*, let us hold firmly to the faith we profess." The juxtaposition of these two names is instructive and compelling. He is Jesus, the human person, able to sympathize with our weaknesses (v. 15). Chapter 2 of this epistle is a masterful exposition of the true and representative humanity of Jesus, who became human, lived and died vicariously for us. Chapter 5 provides knowledge that is not recorded in the Gospels, that Jesus experienced "strong crying and tears" as he lived out his life in solidarity with humanity's pain and in anticipation of his vicarious suffering for humanity's sin— and death, its consequence. This man, the man who became one with us, has cried; and this man, with whom we have become one by regeneration, cries with us in our losses and in our grief. We "never walk alone" when we go through trials and losses.

Yet he is not just a man! He is, according to this text, the "Son of God." Actually able to give strength, as well as to sympathize. Chapter 1 of this epistle gives the most compelling evidence that Jesus was in fact God, the person in the Trinity eternally predestined to become human, yet the God whose throne is forever and ever (1:8). He represents us before his Father in heaven, as a man, yet he is completely in eternal union and communion with the Father in responding to our needs. Sympathetic and strong to carry us through the valleys, and sympathetic and strong to transform us on the grief journey. We access that sympathy and that strength through prayer ("Let us then approach God's throne of grace with confidence," v. 16), prayer that is initiated and enabled by Christ, who intercedes for us. In the *practices* section below, we will expand on this.

I cannot tell you the number of times I have wished for both sympathy and strength to share at a hospital bedside as a pastor. Sympathy comes relatively easily for me. I enter the situation and the person's feelings easily—perhaps rather too easily, as I am perhaps over-sensitive (my differentiation could be better!). But I have often longed for strength. To be able to impart divine healing, to be able to impart courage that comes from God. My only solace has been to pray in the Spirit, to invoke the name of Jesus, so that *his* strength and *his* sympathy might be imparted through my prayers and the reading of timely Scriptures. I *do* pray for healing, but I also pray for strength for the journey irrespective of the answer to that prayer. I have often wondered why God did not seem to answer my prayers for Sharon's healing. I have come to see that just as much glory is brought to God, and just as much of the influence of grace is brought to people, by someone who suffers well—as she did—than by healing.

I will not forget to my dying day the journey of little Nicholas. It was impossible not to feel deep sympathy for him, for his mom and dad, Charlotte and Alan Merrick, and his siblings, as this cute blonde three-year-old battled leukemia. Never have I prayed so hard than as a pastor journeying with this family, in that little ward in the Vancouver Children's Hospital. One day in particular I had a sense of outrage that this should be happening. I got down on my knees by his bedside with my hand on his little fevered head, crying out to God fervently, pleading for a miracle. The healing was not forthcoming. He died a day later. The strength came to his parents, who endured such a loss with bravery and grace. The strength came to me, enabling me to conduct one of the most difficult memorial services of my pastoral life. It was laced with the peace and ultimate triumph of God, but I felt the weight of such a loss—the loss of a child so young. It's not the way it's supposed to be. But I know that Christ was present, by the Spirit in that room, weeping with Al and Charlotte. And his strength was palpable in their demeanor on that day, and in their journey through the days of grieving that lay in front of them. Whatever little I did as a pastor was only valuable because they already had "first-order relationship" with the Christ of comfort. They were grounded in deep meaning.

How does one equip people to die well, and to grieve well when loved ones die? Ultimately by encouraging them in their connection with the Christ of sympathy and strength. By encouraging them with the reality that whether they suffer as *humans*, as is the common lot of all humans, or as *Christians* in persecution, we suffer in participation—that is, in *koinōnia*—with Christ, and in so doing we get to know Christ even more intimately. This is the meaning of Philippians 3:10–11: "I want to know Christ—yes, to know the power of his resurrection and participation (*koinōnian*) in his sufferings, becoming like him in his death, and so, somehow, attaining to the resurrection from the dead." For Paul, suffering was an ever-present reality of human and Christian life; to know Christ was to know Christ's presence to him in suffering. We equip ourselves and others to grieve and suffer well by encouraging whatever practices are necessary to enhance the communion we have with the Triune God, who beckons them into his own perichoretic life. We will consider these practices in a later chapter.

Melissa Kelley's way of saying the same thing is to encourage people in their attachment to God. She and other advocates[8] of attachment theory have suggested a parallel between human attachment to other humans and human attachment to God. Kelley speaks of ways in which attachment to God either corresponds to that of attachment to parents or support persons, or is compensatory where these attachments have been inadequate.[9] The idea that we attach to God similarly to how we attach to our primary loved ones is a notion James Houston proposed a number of years before attachment theory was well known. In *The Transforming Friendship*, he maintains that people find it difficult to pray because prayer is a friendship with God, and people in general have poor relationship skills. He reflects a reality that may at first seem counterintuitive, that the measure of our intimacy with God is our intimacy with our best human friends or spouse.[10] However, Houston suggests that when people start to pray, that is to simply be in relational intimate communion with God, their human relationships begin to be transformed. By sovereign grace, our relational skills and bonding can be transcended. Persons who have not bonded well with their parents still may discover a deep bond with Christ and their heavenly Father, one that equips them for the possibility of healing broken bonds with parents and other loved ones. One that in times of the loss of our closest friends, in death or divorce, sustains us and compensates.

Kelley describes the comfort of God in a moving way when she writes that in our grieving, God is at work "holding us in our brokenness and facilitating wholeness in a variety of ways." Her book ends with the affirmation that God, "the Master Artist, is constantly at work in all our lives, bringing hope out of brokenness, in love. All will be well."[11]

In our next chapter we explore how this attachment or communion with God is enabled through the life of prayer, which enables reconstruction and transformation even in the midst of grief.

---

8. She draws especially on the work of Lee Kirkpatrick—"Attachment and Religious Representations and Behavior" and *Attachment, Evolution and the Psychology of Religion*.

9. Kelley, *Grief*, 62.

10. See Houston, *Transforming Friendship*. This is in keeping with the sentiments of 1 John, which in many different ways makes the point that loving our brother/sister or neighbor, and loving God, are mutually interconnected and interactive. 1 John 4:20 makes this most clear: *"For if we do not love a fellow believer, whom we have seen, we cannot love God, whom we have not seen."*

11. Kelley, *Grief*, 141.

chapter 9

Moving towards Adaptation—

GRIEF SHARING WITH THE TRIUNE GOD
IN RECONSTRUCTION

Union with (Attachment to) the Triune God

. . . That Forms Strength and Character (Reconstruction in the
Prolonged Phase of Grief)

IN THE ACUTE PHASE of my grieving, my sense of the loss of a home was deep. By the grace of God, I did not lose hope. This hope was accentuated by "visions" I experienced on two different occasions while listening to songs of worship. One was of Sharon lying prostrate before the Lamb in abject adoration and worship. In the other, I saw her standing at heaven's door when it came time for me to arrive, and of course, she had her arms stretched wide. "Welcome home honey!" she said. Jesus was standing just behind her, and although of course it will be first and foremost about seeing him and his glory, it was as if Jesus had let Sharon get in the first welcome.

That conjured up two images for me. One was of watching Sharon's favorite clip of Princess Diana welcoming her two young boys on the royal yacht Britannia, after she had been away from them for a long while. Her arms were outstretched as she got down on her knees, and her boys ran into those arms. But this image also reminded me of the times when I had been away when our kids were young. As I arrived in the car and Sharon came to the door, she would always let Martyn and Heather run to me first. She could wait to give me her hug until she'd first had the pleasure of seeing her children run into the arms of their father. In my vision it was definitely a Sharon hug, with both arms extended all the way. I was *home*.

The metaphor of *home* is apt with respect to finding and practicing the intimacy with God that fosters attachment to him, bringing comfort and strength—and then to the kind of change that God redemptively works in us. We often think of the passing-on of loved ones as their "going home," and there is good biblical precedent for this. Paul speaks plainly in 2 Corinthians 5 of the reality that death would result in his (and for all people who die knowing Christ) being "*at home with the Lord*" (5:8). But there is a real sense in which even in this life we can know what it means to find our home in the Triune God, even if the ultimate and full experience awaits the life to come. God is not called "Father" in the New Testament by accident. The filial or familial metaphor is the dominant one for describing the people of God. This dynamic of finding our home in God is a central spiritual motif.

For example, speaking of those who love him—that is, of those who have the Spirit—Jesus says in John 14:23, "*My Father will love them and we will come to them and make our home with them.*" Peter's language is that of participating in the divine nature, not by becoming God, but by relationally entering and experiencing his life (2 Pet 1:4).

Coming to faith in Christ is a welcoming home, just as in the Parable of the Prodigal Son. He was welcomed with open arms by his father, who stood on tiptoe and then ran to embrace him. We become children of God, joint heirs with Christ of the kingdom of God. However, this initiating event is followed by a life of coming home, of entering it more fully, of imbibing the triune love more deeply. Paul depicts this process in his greatest prayer in Ephesians 3:14–21.

> For this reason I kneel before the Father, from whom every family in heaven and on earth derives its name. I pray that out of his glorious riches he may strengthen you with power through his Spirit in your inner being, so that Christ may dwell in your hearts through faith. And I pray that you, being rooted and established in love, may have power, together with all the Lord's holy people, to grasp how wide and long and high and deep is the love of Christ, and to know this love that surpasses knowledge—that you may be filled to the measure of all the fullness of God. Now to him who is able to do immeasurably more than all we ask or imagine, according to his power that is at work within us, to him be glory in the church and in Christ Jesus throughout all generations, for ever and ever! Amen.

We find a wonderful sense of co-participation (reflecting the co-inherence, or perichoresis) of the persons of the Trinity in this prayer, such that in praying to the Father, the Spirit strengthens us and facilitates the presence of Christ in our hearts, and the end-product is the fullness of the whole Godhead! However, we also see a distinctness of the persons. Specifically, we are encouraged to pray to the Father.

Jesus himself taught us this. When you pray, he told his disciples, say, *"Our Father . . . ."* But Jesus introduced us into the precious intimacy conveyed in the term "Father," not just by teaching, but by example. Jesus always prayed to his Father, because that was and is who he is! As Karl Barth has pointed out, "God is Father because and insofar as Jesus Christ is his Son and He is the Father of Jesus Christ."[1] We call God "Father" because we have entered in to the Son by union with him. Thus, Barth adds, "our freedom to call upon God as Father is grounded absolutely in the way in which Jesus Christ called upon him, and still does so, when he turns to him."[2] Barth also suggests that Christians call God by the vocative "Father" in invocation (the principal rubric for the Christian life for Barth), "apart from and in spite of what they deserve," and that they do so only because "by Jesus Christ and through his Spirit they have been taken up into *his* invocation of God as *his* Father."[3] He suggests therefore that the Christian cannot ever pray to the Father without consciousness that he/she does so by grace, and therefore with consciousness that we as the church are a "prophetic minority" with responsibility for mission—the bringing of others into that relationship with "Abba."

This most grace-filled core concept of biblical revelation, that God is *Father*, is crucial to our healing from grief over the long term and to our reconstruction. This title of Father assumes his providence in all the circumstances of our lives, but it also is a term of great gentleness that answers to our greatest hungers and longings as human daughters and sons. We long for his embrace, and we can run to him and find in him the love we miss and long for. There are great depths to probe here. We are always only infants in the things of God; that is, in spirituality or our spiritual pilgrimage. The prayer of St. Catherine of Siena to the Trinity is appropriate here:

1. The references in this paragraph to sections of the *Church Dogmatics* are as cited in an essay entitled "Karl Barth on the Lord's Prayer" by Donald K. McKim, in Saliers (ed.), *Prayer: Barth,* 118–20.

2. Barth, *The Christian Life,* CD IV/4: Lecture Fragments, 65.

3. Ibid., 100.

"O abyss! O eternal Godhead! O deep sea! What more could you have given me than the gift of your very self!"[4]

The key to transformation in the midst of grieving, if one can even think of transformation, is not to be preoccupied with transformation, because we shall thereby become anthropocentric and self-obsessed. Transformation happens imperceptibly, as we begin to be preoccupied with God and plunge into the deep sea of his love and participate in his divine life. In that divine triune life—in which essentially, each is "for the other" and "towards the other"—there is room for us. Hurting human persons have been brought into that circle of intimacy by amazing grace, because we are in Christ—who participated in humanity that humans might participate in God. He takes us up with all our burdens and all our grief, and having assured us of his deep sympathy—gained in the darkest sufferings imaginable—he draws us into the arms of the Father.

This invitation to grieving people, to enter (when they are ready) into a deep life in God, might seem callous, but let us explore the great reality revealed in this great Pauline prayer: all prayer, and every entry into comforting communion with God, is completely graced. It is enabled by the Triune God himself. We can only pray as he is praying in us. Christians regrettably think of salvation as by faith, and of prayer and spirituality as by works. In fact, with a posture of openness to God, he himself enables us to pray. We pray, but only as he is praying. His praying and our praying are compatible. This is a kind of asymmetric compatibilism, by which God prays and we pray too.

The first three petitions of this engraced prayer, which describe the pilgrimage into God that grief and suffering can precipitate, belong together: Paul asks that the Father would strengthen the inner being of each Christian by the Spirit for the realized indwelling of Christ, in order that the experience of immeasurable love might bring them into the fullness of God. Note that invocation of the Father results in the action of all three persons of the Trinity. And each person of the Trinity ultimately enables one and the same thing.

The location referred to, within the human person, is the same in each of the second and third phrases: into the "inner man" (penetrating into), which is the "heart" (the seat of the intellect, affection, and imagination). The strengthening of the Spirit and the resultant indwelling of Christ refer to the same experience, in that the Spirit's indwelling is what imparts the

---

4. Catherine of Siena, *The Dialogue*, dialogue 167.

indwelling of Christ. Remember, the Spirit is the Spirit of Christ—without whom no person is a believer, according to Romans 8:9–10. This is true to what Jesus predicted in John 14:15–18: *"If you love me, you will obey what I command. And I will ask the Father, and he will give you another Counselor to be with you forever—the Spirit of truth. The world cannot accept him, because it neither sees him nor knows him. But you know him, for he lives with you and will be in you. I will not leave you as orphans; I will come to you."* It is reflective of a reality that trinitarian theologians have referred to as *perichoresis* or coinherence, by which the presence and attributes of one Person in the Godhead are made present by the presence of an Other. Here the Father's invocation generates the Spirit, who mediates the presence of Christ to the heart of the believer by his strengthening presence in the inner person. In fact, Jesus indicated that the Spirit's indwelling would convey not only the presence of the Son, but also the Father, in John 14:20, 23. *"On that day you will realize that I am in my Father, and you are in me, and I am in you. . . . Jesus replied, 'If anyone loves me, he will obey my teaching. My Father will love him, and we will come to him and make our home with him.'"* The Son cannot be present without the Father. In fact—and this is the perspective of Western Trinitarianism—the Spirit is in fact the mutual love of the Father for the Son and the Son for the Father. The Spirit sheds the love of God abroad in our hearts (Rom 5:5), but that love is the love of the Father for the Son.

Thus, worship, including prayer, becomes, as James B. Torrance states it, "the gift of participating through the Spirit in the Incarnate Son's communion with the Father."[5] It is not initiated by us, but by the Father himself—as John 4:23 indicates, *"they are the kind of worshipers the Father seeks."* Prayer is not initiated by us; it is a response to the intercessions of the incarnate Christ, an entering into his vicarious life of worship and intercession. As Torrance puts it, prayer is "our liturgical amen to the worship of Christ."[6] It is thus *incarnational* trinitarian prayer. And we enter into that response by the work of the Holy Spirit within us. "We do not know what we ought to pray for, but the Spirit himself intercedes for us with groans that words cannot express" (Rom 8:26b; cf. Rom 8:34; Heb 7:25). It is thus *pneumatological* trinitarian prayer. Again, Torrance states:

> The first real step on the road to prayer is to recognize that none of us knows how to pray as we ought. But as we bring our desires

5. Torrance, *Worship, Community*, 20.

6. Ibid., 14.

to God, we find that we have someone who is praying for us, with us, and in us. Thereby he teaches us to pray and motivates us to pray, and to pray in peace to the Lord. Jesus takes our prayers—our feeble, selfish, inarticulate prayers—he cleanses them, makes his prayers, and in a "wonderful exchange"—he makes his prayers our prayers and presents us to the Father as his dear children, crying: "Abba Father."[7]

When strength is weak and fatigue is great, as often is the case for grieving people, we are somehow more receptive to this kind of contemplative prayer: prayer as participation in God, prayer dependent on the Spirit, prayer that is a leaning on God, more listening to him than petitioning him, more responding to him than asking him. When we pray with our own self-effort, we remove prayer from the context of grace and it can become legalistic, empty, ritualistic, and self-focused. This dynamic understanding of prayer and worship frees us from the banality of always focusing on the quality of experience we have as we pray and worship—which is just as well when we are grieving. God has created us for communion with himself, and he has so pre-ordered communion that it is possible for us with all our sin and weakness. God has made prayer to be a gift of grace. Gift is prior to task. If this were not so, prayer would be a graceless attempt to fulfill the purpose for which we were created. That we worship and pray at all is a gift from the Triune God of grace, and we in turn offer it back to him. And it is so sanctified by the Son and the Spirit that it is acceptable to the Father.

The Trinity is thus the very grammar of prayer, which is the grammar of grace. We pray according to the riches of the grace of the Triune God. God graciously descends to us, and through this grace, we ascend to God in worship and prayer. Prayer inheres in the communion the Son has with the Father. It is not something that occurs "outside" God. It is true communion with God, communion with God as he is in himself.

Especially notice the term in this prayer, "*may dwell.*" Clearly, Paul is speaking to Christians who already know the indwelling of Christ by the Spirit in their lives. The same verb is actually used in 2:22 of God's dwelling in his people as his temple. The verb "live" or "dwell" reveals two nuances here. First, the verb conveys more than a temporary lodging (that would be the Greek word *paroikeō*), but rather, the concept of a permanent and comfortable dwelling (*katoikeō*). The verb can be translated "*make his home*" in your hearts. It has OT background; its root idea is that of the design

7. Ibid., 45–46.

of the temple, so that God may inhabit it.[8] Second, this verb's form, and specifically its aorist tense, is significant. The aorist tense is much abused in Christian interpretation; it does not in and of itself imply a "crisis never to be repeated," but it is simply the "point" tense that indicates an event that occurs (it can also recur). It is in one sense an unremarkable tense when used here; this is how Paul would normally describe events. He surely has in mind a definite act by which Christ indwells. He does not mean, however, that this is a "once for all" mystical experience.

I want to suggest that Paul has in mind the *subjective sense* of that indwelling, and in particular the formation of Christ within us, which happens again and again. After all, it happens in our *"hearts."* Bear in mind the way Paul prays for the Galatians: *". . . until Christ be formed in you."* Every Christian is indwelt by Christ; still, there are specific times when that indwelling is "experienced," and there are events in our spiritual formation that increase the measure in which Christ is "at home" in our hearts, whether we feel them or not. Every Christian is in union with Christ, but not every Christian at every moment has the same degree of experienced communion with Christ. Paul seems to be praying for a fresh encounter and formative work of Christ in their hearts, something we are always in need of. It seems that seasons of grief and suffering, which make us vulnerable and soft, are exactly the times when we are most likely to enter into this prayer.

Furthermore, the connotation of this indwelling is that Christ has free reign of the heart. In other words, when Christ comes, he comes as Lord to reign. In certain seasons of our lives, an intense degree of "soul work" is being done in us. This is what Paul prays for here: A fresh awareness of the presence and reign of Christ within us may mark our permitting his presence in as-yet-unopened wounds and areas of struggle, and our allowing him to impart his gentle correction and healing affection. Bishop Handley Moule states that at any stage of the Christian life we are in need of that fresh awareness, a "new arrival and entrance"[9] of Christ within us. Moule notes: "Local images are always elastic in the spiritual sphere; and there is no contradiction thus in the thought of the permanent presence of One who is yet needed to arrive."[10]

8. Eadie, *Commentary on the Epistle of Paul to the Ephesians,* 247.

9. Moule, *Studies in Ephesians,* 97.

10. Ibid.

Paul prays that the Father might give to the saints a deeper, more manifest sense of the Savior's residence as Lord/ruler and lover of their souls, one that might at first be exposing and purifying, but then healing. It would "strangely warm" their hearts as it caused them to be "rooted and grounded" in love.

In the course of my preaching life, I have been entertained in many homes. In some I felt fully at home, with full freedom to access the fridge or the TV room. In others, I felt I couldn't touch anything and retreated to my bedroom for respite. Paul's prayer is that the Savior would be at home within us with full freedom. Having been a missionary kid who traveled and lived in many countries, I have thought a lot about the concept of "home" over the years. It has been, I admit, a painful concept, since I was not well grounded in that experience. I went from home to home in Angola, in Scotland (always referred to as "home" by my parents), Angola, boarding school in Zambia, Scotland again, Zimbabwe, South Africa, Kingston (Ontario), Dallas (Texas), Scotland yet again, England, and then Canada again—Kingston, Burnaby, Port Coquitlam, Montreal, White Rock, and now Vancouver. My years in Scotland between ages seven and nine were my happiest, and I still think of Scotland as home.

But this is probably more of a romantic notion than a reality. In 2004, after defending my theology PhD thesis, I stood watching a rugby match in Galashiels, one of Scotland's border towns. There in the midst of a boisterous crowd (the farewell game for Gary Armstrong and Doddie Weir, two of Scotland's rugby greats) as foul farm smells wafted across the stadium, I began thinking about the concept of home. Why did I feel so at home here? Perhaps I needed to go back to Canada and tell Sharon and our children that we should live in Scotland. Yet I knew what Sharon's reaction would be: "You'll be going on your own!" Anyway, our children were Canadians. And as I was thinking these thoughts, the Spirit of God spoke to me in a way that moved me deeply, in what seemed like an audible voice within: "Ross, I am your home."

Suddenly there I stood, watching a rugby match with tears in my eyes. The person I had come with might have thought I was grieving the retirement of those rugby players! But no, this was far deeper—I was sensing the presence and love of Christ within me. It was one of those moments I believe Paul refers to in Ephesians 3. The experience brought some healing for my lack of groundedness as a person, which has often manifested itself in restlessness that is hard to be around (ask my poor wife)!

Thus, engraced and participatory prayer is crucial in encountering and receiving the God of all comfort. In a subsequent chapter, we will speak more of other spiritual practices, first of a communal nature—that is, in the life of the church and then in human community in general. Then we will consider personal practices. But first, at a more intellectual level, we will look at the matter of theodicy, the defense of the goodness of God in light of the presence of metaphysically and morally evil events. After all, the questions will come around in the minds of most grieving people: Why? And where was God? Where *is* God?

chapter 10

Moving towards Adaptation

THEODICY OF THE TRIUNE GOD WHO SUFFERS

THE SHARING OF GOD in human grief is the best of all theodicy arguments. Other books give a more extensive coverage of theodicy arguments,[1] which seek to account for the existence of evil and suffering in the world, as well as in the personal lives of human beings. When the Triune God created the cosmos, he did so in such a way that he was distinct from his creation (i.e., creation is at some "metaphysical remove"[2] from its Creator). The act of creation was not an extension of God's being, but the product of his will. To say it another way, God created in freedom. Creation was not necessary, but an overflow of the infinite richness of the extravagant love and beauty that eternally characterized his own inner life. The agency of the pre-incarnate Son in creation (John 1:3; Col 1:16; Heb 1:2–3) ensured that the creation maintained its metaphysical distance from God and, at the same time, it assured God's relational nearness and engagement with the universe in every moment of time. Thereby all created substances, though dependent on God, were granted freedom to have their own existence (though a contingent existence) and were to be involved to some extent in their own destiny.

This is an important element for a theodicy: creation was a kenotic act on God's behalf even before the incarnation. Perhaps both went together in God's eternal purposes, given the seminal place of the incarnation and resurrection in the formation of the new creation from the old.

---

1. See for example, Zylla, *Roots of Sorrow*; Oden, *Pastoral Theology,* 223–48.
2. Polkinghorne, *Science and the Trinity,* 164.

As scientist-theologian John Polkinghorne states, "The existence of free creatures is a greater good than a world populated by perfectly behaving automata." However, Polkinghorne also notes "that good has the cost of mortality and suffering."[3] This leads him to speak of the transformation of the old creation into the new, the second stage of God's creation: its re-demption and reconciliation by Christ, creation not *ex nihilo*, but *ex vetere*.

Why does it happen in this way? What is the purpose of this old creation? The answer lies partly in the freedom spoken of, and the conse-quences of such freedom. Another answer lies in the fact that somehow, in the providence of God, more grace and more glory is revealed of the God who redeems a contingent universe than one who creates perfect automata. And more glory still is brought to God by his entrance into this fallen humanity in the incarnation of the Man of Sorrows, acquainted with grief.

So God's profound engagement with creation and humanity in its fall-enness, to reconcile and redeem it, is the mysterious reality of the Christian gospel of a God who suffers with his creation—and particularly with the pinnacle of his creation, his image-bearers. The incarnation and vicarious humanity and resurrection of Christ, in which the fallen creation was re-newed and the creation reaffirmed, is crucial in this. The cross of Christ, where he suffered all the abandoned God-forsakenness of the fallen cre-ation, is at the center of this. God in Christ, by an act of the will in full free-dom, suffered vicariously for us, to reconcile and redeem not only humans but the whole universe (Col 1:19–20). This argument may not convince everyone, but the grief-sharing of the Triune God with us, and for us, goes a long way in that direction for me.

It is one thing to have some sense of the goodness of God in a broad-world sense. It is yet another to believe God is good when my loved one is dying, or has been killed in a freak accident. That is to have a personal theo-dicy, even if it is a humble and provisional one. When we encounter per-sonal tragedy, we are naturally prone to ask *why*, or why *my* child, or why *me*? When we care for grieving people, that question of purpose, "Where is God now?" inevitably comes up. Simplistic answers must be avoided, and yet they abound in the Christian world. My wife Tammy takes some comfort knowing that her beloved husband's season in palliative care was used by God for bringing to faith his friend Warren, and his gaining assur-ance of eternal life in Christ. However, this does not lead to the conclusion that this was the reason Carlos was taken at the prime of life, taken from his

3. Ibid., 165.

children so that he would never see their graduations, their driving license triumphs, their weddings, or his grandchildren.

Cornelius Plantinga's book on theodicy is aptly titled *Not the Way It's Supposed to Be*.[4] In the beginning of time, humanity used its freedom to lived independently of God. Humanity is thus fallen, and creation with it. Christ as the last Adam, the prototypical and representative man, came into this fallen humanity and creation in order to reconcile it to God. He dealt the death blow to suffering and death in his own death (Heb 2:14; Col 2:14–15). As a result, everyone who believes in Christ and is made one with him is released from the slavery that the fear of death brings.

However, despite death having been dealt the death blow—the crucial victory in the war—the war is not over. Death, which Paul calls "the last enemy to be destroyed," continues until the second coming of Christ and the fulfillment of the new creation, in which "there will be no more death." Until that time, there are tears, mysteries, losses, sadness, and tragedy. When that day comes, what Christ has accomplished by his death and resurrection will finally effectuate the "death of death," and then, *"he will wipe every tear from their eyes"* (Rev 21:4). In the "in-between" time, tears are the order of the day. The reasons why Carlos was permitted to pass on may include this redemptive moment in Warren's life, but most of the reasons are beyond our current knowledge. The sentiments of the old hymn, written by Charles A. Tindley (1905) and popularized by Elvis, "We will understand it better by and by" may sound clichéd, but they are true.

In Sharon's illness and ultimate passing, I was not prone to asking "Why me?" At least not during her illness or immediately following her death. Having seen so many people in the congregations I have served pass away from cancer, it was almost a question of "Why *not* me?" Why shouldn't I suffer like everybody else? It is possible to stand aloof from suffering humanity, to have an imbedded belief that this happens to others, not me. I confess to having experienced some of these prideful sentiments earlier in life. In the midst of this harrowing experience of the illness and passing of my beloved, by Christ's grace at work within me, I was freshly welcomed into humanity. Those were the exact words my psychiatrist used when I felt ashamed of being depressed: "Welcome to humanity." I was typical of academic people, who often stay aloof from relationships and the awkward business of feelings. Depression and its treatment had helped me enter into

---

4. See Plantinga, *Not the Way It's Supposed to Be*.

humanity. Sharon's death was, in a very deep way, a further entering into broken and fragile humanity.

In her years as an ICU nurse, Sharon had also seen many people die; she did not ask "Why me?" either. Her attitude combined her level of hope regarding her departure to be with Christ, her memories of her much-loved dad who had gone before, and the realism that becomes ingrained in nurses: people in this fallen world, this "now but not yet" stage of the kingdom of God, get ill and have accidents, and they die. Comparing one's lot with the lot of others is not a means to avoid facing one's own grief and pain, but it does provide perspective. Growing up in Africa, I saw poverty and widespread disease and suffering. The way we die in rich Western countries is anesthetized and sanitized in ways the two-thirds world knows nothing of.

Not that any blame may be assigned to those who do ask "why." The poetic literature of the Old Testament is fraught with protestation, questioning, and lament. These are records of the prayers of godly people, whose relationship with God was real enough that they could ask "why"—sometimes in hot anger. I definitely had days like that, whether or not an "anger phase" of grieving exists. Those days included many of the "This is not the way it's supposed to be" moments. Both our children graduated within a year after Sharon died. Our son Martyn walked a long way in an outdoor ceremony the day he graduated from university, and so I had plenty of time to watch him walk, fully conscious that his mom should have been there. The mom who raised him and delighted in him, and watched pretty much all of his rugby matches with me, shouting herself hoarse. She should have been there! Similarly, our daughter Heather walked on crutches across the stage when she graduated, because she had just broken her ankle in a car crash. Her crutches added visual symbolism to the already charged and forlorn situation. At her wedding a few years later, I wept all the way down the aisle. Even when moms are alive, this is an emotional event for a dad. Her absence made it more poignant. Sharon just should have been there. It's *not* the way it's supposed to be.

The years have not greatly ameliorated this aspect of grief. Roughly four years after Sharon died, Martyn won a provincial and national journalistic award for a story he wrote and broadcast about a Kamloops Blazers hockey player who almost lost his mother in a car accident, in which he himself was also badly injured. As Martyn asked the player what it was like to see his mom next to him in the car, badly injured, looking like she was not going to make it, the player broke down in the interview. A true professional, Martyn said nothing in the interview about how he actually lost his mom. For those who knew, this made the interview especially moving. Tammy and I were invited to the awards dinner in Burnaby, and we found to our surprise that we were in the midst of a Who's Who of newscasters and journalists in the province. There were only about fifty people there. When it came time for Martyn to receive his award, he made a five-minute speech with great competence that ended this way: "I want to thank my dad and his wife Tammy, and I want to dedicate this award to my mom." I cried copious tears. He sat down in the seat beside me afterward, and I put my arm around him and told him how proud I was of him, and we both wept. Oh yes, she should have been there!

Something in me gets triggered just seeing our children ever since Sharon died. I am sure I project my own emotions as I imagine their sense of vast loss. When they are in any challenging situation, this is exacerbated. My anger rises up easily, and it is not necessarily rational. I find myself saying to Sharon, sometimes out loud, "Where are you? I need you here! Why did you leave us?"

So what is the redemptive reality that is implied in all this? "It's not the way it's supposed to be" implies a day when all that is supposed to be, *will be*. Certainly we trust, in faith, that the hope of resurrection and the new creation will make sense of the grief we experience in this life. Having spoken in a previous chapter of the presence of God to us now, in this life, in our sorrow and pain, I will not major on that theme here. But two aspects of a theodicy of God's grief-sharing with us here, now, provide some comfort.

The Refinement Suffering Brings

The first aspect is the transformation that God effects within us through the refinement that suffering brings. In the economy of the God who chooses to create, knowing that he must enter creation and suffer with and for it, and so gain the best of all possible ways of being glorious; and in the economy of the Son of God who is perfected for his role as redeemer through suffering (Heb 5:8–9), humans also suffer. And although God is not the efficient cause of suffering, he uses it in the lives of his people to build character and to make them Christ-like. The fellowship of Christ's sufferings makes us like him in his death (Phil 3:10). That is, it can produce in us a posture of complete devotion to the Father, and submissiveness to his will.

Two things need to be said about this: (i) This does not mean that God is sadistic, and it does not mean that we are masochistic. The suffering caused by evil was not directly willed by God, but in his magnanimous love and by his humble grace, he eternally planned to redeem it. Suffering in our lives happens because we live in a fallen world that still awaits full redemption. We don't go looking for it. But when it comes, with the right orientation towards it and towards God, good can come of it. That brings me to the second point: (ii) The fruitfulness of our grief and our suffering is conditional upon our orientation or posture towards God, and towards it, and towards the purpose of our own refining. In Hebrews 12:11, in the context of speaking about the role of hard times in the formation of the sons and daughters of their loving Father—with strong realism—the author says, *"No discipline seems pleasant at the time, but painful."* The context reveals a corrective role in suffering.

However, the author continues with these words of encouragement concerning the fecundity of these experiences. *"Later on, however, it produces a harvest of righteousness and peace . . . ."* This encourages us. In ways we may not even see, we are being transformed by our losses and grief processing. Loss of loved ones especially heightens one's sensitivity to eternal realities and to the shortness of life, leading to a renewal of devotion in the rest of the life that God gives us. But it also causes Christ to be present to us in unusually real ways, if we are attentive. And notice how this verse ends: this productivity of the graces of *"righteousness and peace"* in our lives is conditional upon the meaning of this phrase: *". . . for those who have been trained by it."* It is sometime translated *"exercised by it."* This is a gymnasium word. Soul exercises are required to make suffering fruitful.

We will explore some of those exercises in the next two chapters, but by way of summary, all these are seen with a view to participating in the life of God by grace, and they are all enabled by God's prevenient grace. They are not a set of hoops to climb through in order to merit communion with God or his approval, or to bring about some change of character. Rather, they are ways of being attentive to God, ways of giving space for communion with Christ, ways of enabling mindfulness to the voice of God enabled by the Holy Spirit. The previous verse sets the tone for this emphasis. Notice that God does this work of grace in us by our participation in *his* holiness: *"God disciplines us for our good, in order that we may share in his holiness"* (Heb 12:10).

We cannot forget that although we are loved more deeply than we can ever know by God, nevertheless "discipleship" means that we are under Christ's discipline. He works in all our circumstances, and especially our hurts and tragedies, to prepare us not only for this life but for the life to come. We turn to that life to come now.

The Resurrection Hope

A hope that rings faintly in the Old Testament but comes to fruition and re-sounds in the New is the hope of the resurrection of the people of God, and their inhabiting a new creation in which there is no more pain, no more death, no more tears. This hope sustains us in our deepest losses and when we hear of the greatest tragedies of injustice and cruelty in this life. The story isn't over yet. The last word has not yet been given about injustice or pain. That word is reserved for the One entered into our pain, endured all grief, and who by dying conquered death. We often express our judgments about whether the world is fair, and whether a God who is all-loving and all-powerful can possibly be just. But our judgments are premature. God will make all things new. All things will, in the end, be put right.

This hope, which involves seeing Christ and seeing our loved ones in resurrected bodies, is the reason Paul can be confident that Christians, though they do grieve, need not grieve with utter hopelessness: *"Brothers and sisters, we do not want you to be uninformed about those who sleep in death, so that you do not grieve like the rest of mankind, who have no hope"* (1 Thess 4:13). Let me attempt a brief summary of the personal eschatology of Christian faith.

To adapt the words of Winston Churchill, "Death is not the end. It is not even the beginning of the end, though it may be the end of the beginning." Contrary to the dualistic way in which today's society, influenced by Greek philosophy, sees human persons, they do not *have* a body. They *are* an animated body, a body animated by the life or soul God has given them (not "a body housing a soul"). After they die, when Christ returns (and we won't enter into the discussion of when that will happen or what it leads to—that broader eschatology is beyond our scope here!), they will be resurrected and once again be living, integrated body-soul, whole persons.

There are some things we can know from the fact that Christ as the God-Man is linked to humanity and with creation. The first is that just as he has an embodied existence as the last Adam, the prototypical human

being, the *"firstborn from the dead,"* to use a Pauline phrase, so we too will
forever be embodied. This is Paul's principal contention in 1 Corinthians
15. It is, however, also in line with what human persons are as animated
bodies, not incarnate souls. Furthermore, Jesus—who is the prototype for
all of us in resurrection (1 Cor 15:13, 20–23)—was physically recognizable
after he rose again.

Identity in those embodied persons will be preserved in a manner that
also distantly echoes the nature of the Triune Godhead in which Christ the
Son—though one eternally with the Father, mutually internal to the Father
and the Spirit—is yet still and eternally possessed of an irreducible identity
as the hypostasis or person of the Son. Personhood is a primary category
in the reality of creation, as it is in the eternal Trinity. It is *personhood-
in-community*, but it is personhood nevertheless. And it is personhood-
in-*community*. Integral to our existence as persons in heaven and when
heaven comes to earth is that we are in community. Human being does not
exist apart from human belonging.

We also see evidence in the Bible of the post-death identity of persons.
For example, Jesus said that God—as the God of the living and not the
dead—is the God of Abraham, Isaac, and Jacob, who apparently still have
their identity. When Moses and Elijah appeared on the Mount of Transfiguration (Matt 17:3–4), they were recognized and acknowledged. I do realize
that the general resurrection, when all will be raised, had not yet happened
when this appearance occurred, but if in this "intermediate state" Moses
and Elijah are Moses and Elijah, then we and our loved ones, when we are
in the intermediate state between death and resurrection and in resurrection, will also have our own identity. The point is that Moses and Elijah
are still *Moses* and *Elijah* after their transportation to heaven. Similarly, all
Christians will one day be transformed into the image of Christ and yet still
be Carlos or Sharon . . . that is, whoever they were on earth.

I believe that like Christ in his pre- and post-resurrection states, there
will be both continuity and discontinuity in resurrected persons compared
to who they were in this life. English scientist-theologian John Polkinghorne suggests that the soul is the *information-bearing pattern* of the body.
In saying this, he is drawing on the ancient concept spoken of by Aristotle
and Aquinas, who believed that the soul is the form or pattern of the body,
but with the significant adaptation that Polkinghorne is speaking of a soul-
body unity, not of a dualistic "soul in a body" entity. Polkinghorne's concept
does not rule out, but rather includes, our physical genome or genetic code,

which is crucial to the body/soul unity that humans are. But Polkinghorne wants especially to insist that this information-bearing pattern must include our relationships, which play so significant a part in the character of our personhood, as well as all the experiences that have shaped our identity. As he notes, "Acknowledgment of this highly complex and multi-dimensional character of the soul avoids the rather too desiccated concept that 'information-bearing pattern' might otherwise be in danger of suggesting."[5]

Thus God, who knows our DNA and our unique history of relationships, will not struggle to raise bodies and reconstitute whole persons from the graves and oceans and hills where their ashes have been scattered. Does this mean that Sharon will have lovely blue eyes, and will they be lovelier still? Will her laugh, so uproarious and infectious, be the same or amplified? If her heart's capacity for caring was so big "down here," will it be even bigger and will God have work for her to do? I suspect so.

We do tend to think about heaven mostly as "up," but it will really be onwards, that is horizontal. The trajectory of God's plan for the world is horizontal, with vertical intervention in the end; that is, God's story is of the creation, fall, and redemption of the world, and then the consummation, which is the transfiguration and restoration of creation, not its destruction. And that new creation is brought about by the coming of heaven to earth. We will have bodies, orientated towards the spiritual yet true to their unique and original creational identity, and we will likely be put to work, because work is what God does. The gift of work, given by the Creator to his image-bearing human creatures, was given before the fall. Therefore, work is something good, and I suspect that in the new creation, we will work without the "thorns and thistles" that make work onerous in this fallen world.

Above all, Jesus the Lamb will be the center and theme of our worship in that new creation. We will know we are made whole and new in him. We will know we have been redeemed, and all the pain in our storms redeemed, in and through him. And I know there will be no more pain; the language of Revelation 21:1–4 is reassuring on that count.

> Then I saw a new heaven and a new earth, for the first heaven and the first earth had passed away, and there was no longer any sea. I saw the Holy City, the new Jerusalem, coming down out of heaven from God, prepared as a bride beautifully dressed for her husband. And I heard a loud voice from the throne saying, "Look!

---

5. Polkinghorne, *Science and the Trinity*, 162.

God's dwelling place is now among the people, and he will dwell with them. They will be his people, and God himself will be with them and be their God. He will wipe every tear from their eyes. There will be no more death or mourning or crying or pain, for the old order of things has passed away."

These realities bring great comfort in the in-between time. As Henry Ward Beecher said, "God washes the eyes by tears until they can behold the invisible land where tears shall come no more."

There are many things about that life that we do not know. Like how previously married people will relate to each other. And what age we will be when we are resurrected and occupy the new earth, after the new Jerusalem comes down to earth. One patristic theologian suggested we'll all be thirty because that's when Jesus began his public ministry, suggesting that this age defines maturity and readiness for service. But we don't really know. This is mystery. Other things are certain. One is that Jesus rose again and that because he was the representative man for humanity, humans will rise again too. They will be in intimate community with him and with one another. Paul says, ". . . *then I shall know fully, even as I am fully known*" (1 Cor 13:12). I love how N. T. Wright expresses this in his book, *Surprised by Hope*:

> All language about the future, as any economist or politician will tell you, is simply a set of signposts pointing into a fog. We see through a glass darkly, says St. Paul as he peers toward what lies ahead. All our language about future states of the world and of ourselves consists of complex pictures that may or may not correspond very well to ultimate reality. But that doesn't mean it's anybody's guess or that every opinion is as good as every other one. And—supposing someone came forward out of the fog to meet us? That, of course, is the central though often ignored Christian belief.[6]

He is of course referring to Jesus, who came to us from out of the fog in resurrection power and told us that because he rose, all in community with him will rise again too! On the last day, Christ will once again come to us from out of the fog, and Christ revealed in the blaze of his glory will remove all fog forever. We will as the redeemed people of God worship the Lamb who was slain for us, and this will be our primary posture as kings and priests, pouring out our praise to God. This posture will orient us towards

---

6. Wright, *Surprised by Hope*, xiii–xiv.

the cultural mandate that was given to the first humans, and which will in the new creation be fulfilled in the new humanity in the last Adam. We will reign as kingly co-creators of a renewed and reconciled creation. We will be priests offering up creation to God in worship. We will work in union with Christ as he reigns over the new earth to which heaven will have come down. The bodies we will have then, as already stated and as confirmed in 1 Corinthians 15, will have continuity with who we are now, as well as significant discontinuity that we do not yet fully grasp. They will be spatially limited, but yet have a spiritual and heavenly orientation we lack now. The soul possesses no inherent immortality (the eternal soul is a Greek concept, not a biblical one). When someone dies, the information-bearing pattern of the soul-body unity would, left to itself, dissolve along with the decaying process. However, crucially, as Polkinghorne adds—and this is a "however" of divine faithfulness, not of naturalistic expectation—"It seems to me to be a perfectly coherent hope to believe that the pattern that is me will be preserved by God at my death and *held in the divine memory* until God's great eschatological act of resurrection, when that pattern will be re-embodied in the 'matter' of the new creation."[7] He then adds, "a credible Christian hope centers on death and resurrection, and not on spiritual survival."

The Intermediate State

This naturally leads to another perennially tough question, especially for those who have lost loved ones, so it is no mere academic exercise for me: where does the person "go" when the soul-body unity decays in the ground or as ashes? While I wish to affirm the broad strokes of Polkinghorne's thesis about how continuity may occur in the new creation, I also want to challenge the now-popular notion that soul-body integrated unity has extinguished all hope that our departed loved ones are in some sense in heaven *now*.

I agree absolutely with the sentiments of N. T. Wright when he emphasizes that resurrection on a new earth is our destiny, and that "going to heaven" is not the ultimate goal, and that therefore the intermediate state is less important and in fact a temporary state on the way to the resurrection state. Wright does not, however, negate the possibility that departed saints are now with Christ in heaven. On the basis of the witness of much Scripture, I wish to be a little more emphatic regarding that, despite the risk

7. Polkinghorne, *Science and the Trinity,* 163.

of appearing to harbor latent Platonic notions as best and gnostic ones at worst.

I recognize that many exegetes and theologians prefer the soul-sleep theory: that when Christians die, their body-soul personhood dies, such that the body in the grave is also the soul in the grave. Those of this school base their preference for this view on an anthropology of the "animated body" variety, rather than the Greek "soul-in-a-body" variety. They rationalize away verses that seem to suggest that Christians upon dying are immediately with the Lord (Phil 1:23 *"I desire to depart and be with Christ, which is better by far;"* 2 Cor 5:8 *"We are confident, I say, and would prefer to be away from the body and at home with the Lord"*), suggesting that from the perspective of the person who dies, they will not know anything until resurrection day, so that from a phenomenological perspective, they will be "immediately" with the Lord when they die.

Beyond the argument that this seems to be very far from "the plain sense of Scripture,"[8] I offer the following arguments for a more obvious interpretation that offers more comfort for grieving people: that the immaterial aspect (soul, spirit) of people who die in Christ really is with the Lord in a direct and intimate way!

i.   Thinking of our loved ones, or less emotively, of human persons just as "information in the divine memory bank" is neither comforting nor true to what persons are.

ii. The idea of the unity of the Persons of the Godhead does not reduce the identity of the divine Persons to such an extent that they cannot be spoken of as acting in a way that is *their own* acting, even if each is in the other in all their actions. So is it possible that in an analogous way, human soul-body unity can exist in a similar fashion? In other words, can the "soul," as indeed Paul seems to speak of it in 2 Corinthians 5, be *absent* from the body but still *belong* together with it for a temporary season when they are not actually together?

iii. The crucial text Polkinghorne and others repeatedly refer to, for evidence of resurrection and the persistence of identity in the kingdom of God—that God is the God of the living and not of the dead, because he is the God now of Abraham, Isaac, and Jacob—seems to

---

8. These same exegetes would (quite rightly, in my books) for the most part react to the "appearance of age" arguments of the literal seven-day creationists in the Genesis account of creation.

me to prove too much, in that Jesus spoke the words of this text in the *present tense*. Furthermore, who are these people, the Elijah and Moses who appear on the Mount of Transfiguration, apparently real and recognizable as persons, even though their resurrection day has not yet come?

iv. What did Jesus mean when he told the dying thief by his side that he would be in paradise with him "*today*" (Luke 23:43)?

v. Why do the psalmist (31:5) and Jesus (Luke 23:46) both speak of their deaths in terms of the dismissal of their spirits to the Father?

vi. What do the texts in the epistles regarding this issue convey when they speak of life after death as a "better state" than now for the departed? Both Philippians 1 and 2 Corinthians 5 may have difficult exegetical elements, but their plain sense seems crystal clear—absence from the body means being in the immediate presence of the Lord.

vii. What does Revelation 6:9–10 mean when it refers to "the souls of those who had been slain" who are present under the heavenly altar and who cry out to God in prayer?

viii. It should also be pointed out that the Christian tradition seems to reflect the view that the saints are conscious in the presence of Christ for as long as Christians have expressed clear views on the question of the conscious state of the dead. The soul-sleep theory is in fact a minority position.

ix. Is this evidence for the tripartite nature of humans? Does the soul-body unity die, but the spirit go to heaven? Is it the spirit rather than the soul that includes the "information-bearing pattern" and which goes to heaven? Why does the writer of Hebrews make so much of the distinction between the spirit and the soul in Hebrews 4:12?

x. If we speak of the human body as dead but actually on this new account mean that the soul/body is dead, what do we mean by a dead *soul*? Death of the soul, it seems to me, is in the NT associated with judgment.

xi. My greatest concern is that we may be doing theology in reaction, or perhaps even in over-reaction, to Platonism and Gnosticism. Theology must ultimately be done in light of the revelation of God personally in Christ, by the Spirit, and in light of the ultimate authority of the Holy Scriptures. It is true that theology has often been clarified in response to heresy, but just because some Christian ideas coincide with Platonic or Neoplatonic ones, this does not necessarily mean they are wrong. At any rate, what I am suggesting—the widely held idea of the immediate presence of the believer in some form in heaven—differs in the following significant ways from a merely Platonic "immortality of the soul" viewpoint:

a. The presence of the soul/spirit in heaven, apart from the dead body of the old creation, does not rule out the possibility that some form of embodiment characterizes the departed person in heaven now, one determined by the same information-bearing pattern held within the divine memory. This seems to have been the case in the appearance of Moses and Elijah.

b. If there is no embodiment of the immaterial part of the human person in heaven now, might it be that this unusual state (i.e., the unusual nature of a "naked" soul) is precisely what draws Paul to comment on it as anomalous in 2 Corinthians 5?

c. Does the fact that in the end, those who die (and those still alive at the *parousia* who are "caught up") will have a future resurrection body and will be integrated body/soul persons, not suffice to vindicate the general Hebrew-Christian anthropology expressed above? To suggest that body and soul *cannot* be separated is to go beyond the statement that they *ought not* to be, or indeed that they are deeply interpenetrated and coinherent. Perhaps we ought to stake our faith in the plain sense of Scripture on this issue and continue to "seek understanding." This would be consonant with our approach to other issues that appear to be inscrutable to this point. For example, when we reach the limits of our understanding of what transpired on the cross in light of the Son's cry of dereliction, and know that the persons of the Trinity can never be metaphysically severed, we reverently rest in the hope of future clarification. We don't negate the truth of the atonement Christ accomplished within the Godhead as our human mediator; nor do we negate the Trinity.

d. A strong theological argument for a present conscious existence of departed Christians is, for me, the communitarian argument—but it is not one I have read or heard of before. It seems to me highly incongruous with the communal nature of human persons that all of a sudden in death they are in an unconscious state, relating to no one. This violates the essence of human personhood as that which is grounded in divine personhood, which is personhood-in-relation. I have no difficulty envisioning departed persons, temporarily as naked souls, communing with each other in heaven—and even more important, in relationship with their Savior. How can we ever envisage a time when people "in Christ" are somehow just "non-existent" to him, in some state of nothingness? This denigrates personhood and violates community. For Paul, death was a state better than life. In fact, whatever it may be, it is better than the goodness of life, but not quite as good as the embodied resurrection state will be. "Good, better, best" is Paul's eschatological trajectory! So if the good state is relational and the best state is relational, how can the intermediate "better" state be isolational and individualistic?

I think it reasonable to assume that somehow, when we let go of our loved ones from our earthly community, they are released into a richer community in heaven with Christ, a community of the worship of the Lamb, which Paul says is better by far. Christians from Eastern Orthodox and Roman Catholic persuasions have a stronger awareness of the presence to the church of those who have gone on before, and who are part of the eternally praising people of God, than those of the Protestant tradition, especially evangelicals. We can learn more than a few things from this ancient tradition.

Having outlined some aspects of the character of God and of Christian theodicy that bring intellectual and effective comfort to grieving people, we come to the communal and personal ways in which grieving people can find comfort in God.

chapter 11

Moving towards Adaptation—

GRIEF SHARING WITH THE *PEOPLE* OF THE TRIUNE GOD (1)

THE CONCEPT OF GRIEF-SHARING includes sharing grief with others—with others in the church in general and with particular others in the church, such as spiritual friends, pastors, and spiritual directors, with counselors and fellow-sufferers who have walked the journey before us or who are walking it now, as well as friends and professionals who are not part of the church, who care for us and our loved ones. In this chapter we consider healing through the corporate nature of the church, including the friendships we develop as ecclesial people; and in the next chapter we'll look at the role of individual persons, pastors, and counselors, who still may be considered part of the ministry of the church.

Healing through the Church

We tend to assume that receiving comfort from God and receiving comfort from being with the people of God are somehow different. Obviously we do distinguish between God and his people, and yet writers of the Bible, like David in Psalm 16, saw the community of God's people and God as one, so that comfort from his people was tantamount to comfort from God. In this psalm, in which the writer is facing death, he speaks of God and his people in parallel:

Keep me safe, *my God*, for in you I take refuge.

I say to the Lord, "You are *my Lord*; apart from you I have no good thing."

I say of the *holy people* who are in the land, "They are the noble ones in whom is all my delight."

The New Testament is even more emphatic regarding this notion that God and his people are relationally one. There are occasions when Paul speaks of Christ meaning "both Christ and his body, together as one entity" (e.g., 1 Cor 12:12). This is not surprising, given that the church is indeed in union with Christ. Multiple metaphors are used to express this in the NT (the Vine and the branches, the Head and the body, the Cornerstone and the temple, the Brother and the family, the Bride and the bridegroom). All this wonderful corporate Christology implies that every Christian is united not only to Christ but to every other child of God in the church universal, and that life together in the local church is the proper expression of this communion. We see no such thing as an unchurched Christian in the New Testament.

The idea of "grief-sharing" is crucial, therefore, not only as a reality between Christ and his people but between persons in his community. There is an important human-human dimension of healing when people share in each others' losses and grief. Of course, this must be textured in a way that honors both the irreducible identity and uniqueness of each person *and* the profound mutuality between human beings, and especially between spiritual friends who are close to the sufferers of loss. This is to say, it honors a truly trinitarian, image-bearing view of anthropology that is neither atomistic and individualistic on the one hand, nor collectivistic on the other. It honors humans as persons-in-community, who reflect analogously the God who is three persons-in-communion. Thus we need to validate both the idiosyncratic nature of each human being in his or her pain and the dynamics of commonality that lead to healing in community.

An example of the idiosyncratic nature of grief is that persons experience grief differently due to their differing cultural heritage. Dale Larson states that a "major development in the field has been increased attention to cultural issues in death, dying, and grief." He cites the work of Paul Rosenblatt, who "uses a plethora of illuminating examples to show how 'culture shapes grieving,'" and convincingly argues that sensitivity to cultural differences, as opposed to "cultural ignorance," is a prerequisite for competent care. His extensive work in this area over four decades has led him to the conclusion that "some aspects of how people grieve may be common across cultures, but it is a mistake to say that all humans grieve in a certain way."[1] Beyond culture, and related to the uniqueness of the personhood of every human being, each one experiences grief in an idiosyncratic way. This must be validated if others are to provide wise help.

Having acknowledged this idiosyncratic aspect, we must also emphasize the importance of community and that there are commonalities to all grieving. The church is God's design for human persons, and although Jesus honored the creation ordinance of family (Matt 15:4), in his call to discipleship in his ministry on several occasions he shockingly relativized the human family, calling people into that more real and enduring family of the people of God, the church (e.g., Mark 10:29). I know of no greater healing for the grieving person than the church of Jesus Christ. Devotion to its practices—the Eucharist, the preaching of the Word, and the fellowship of life together—enables our communion with God, especially during times when personal practices like reading the Scriptures and prayer can be difficult. In an individualistic society that also influences Christian thinking, we tend to greatly value those personal practices or spiritual disciplines, when in fact the New Testament speaks little of these and much of ecclesial practices. Using a striking water analogy, seventeenth-century Church of England Bishop Jeremy Taylor comments on the attendance at temple worship by Mary and Joseph with Jesus: ". . . in public solemnities, God opens his treasures, and pours out his grace, more abundantly. Private devotions, and secret offices of religion, are like refreshing of a garden with the distilling and petty drops of a water-pot; but addresses to the temple, and serving God in the public communion of the saints, is like rain from heaven. . . . For religion is a public virtue; it is the ligature of souls."[2]

Of course, there may be an initial season of acute grief when we cannot participate in the gatherings of the church, but when we are ready, the ecclesial practices of the church will sustain us. As we participate in the Lord's Supper in a regular way, for example, we contemplate the face of Christ who loved us and gave himself for us, who entered into our grief to carry it, who carries us up afresh, with all our sorrows, into the throne of the Father,[3] and who gives us hope. Because we do this only "until he

---

1. Larson, "Taking Stock," 350. For further work on how culture affects grieving, see also Laurie and Neimeyer, "African Americans in Bereavement"; also Lazar and Bjorck, "Religious Support and Psychosocial Wellbeing," 403–21.

2. Taylor, *The Whole Works*, 81.

3. For a rich description of how the Eucharist draws us into the life and comfort of God, see Schmemann, *For the Life of the World*, especially chapter 6.

comes," there will be a day when we and all our loved ones will gather at the Supper of the Lamb. In the meantime we feed on Christ and are formed and strengthened for another week.

As we hear the Word explained and expounded, and the words of man or woman becoming the words of God, in expository preaching, our perspective is recovered. Our faith in the providence of God is restored. Our flighty thoughts, which can lead us into all kinds of tributaries of fear and doubt, are redirected. And as we encounter God and hear the gospel, we are formed afresh. We are exhorted to be faithful, and we are edified, exhorted and *comforted*.

But Word and sacrament are only two of three major marks of the church. Fellowship, *koinōnia*, is the third. The first two occur within a community that shares in Christ and shares out its own life and caring and possessions. Usually, in churches bigger than twenty-five people, this also requires small house churches or cell groups. It is in the context of sharing in these groups that people don't just go to church but start *being* the church. And when people lose loved ones, I have seen these little churches really function as the family of God. In my own experience, the rich community life of the church I had pastored became to me and my family, at the time when we lost our wife and mom, the body of Christ. This was manifested in meals too numerous to mention and by visitors so numerous we couldn't always cope. And in the context of a small group of people I found solace and a place to heal—and distracting fun also!

Larry Crabb, who as a therapist made a pilgrimage from Rational Emotive to Psychodynamic underpinnings, began—while not devaluing therapy—to champion the concept of community as God's primary provision for healing for most people. Speaking of the power of connection between people of the new covenant, Crabb says,

> When two people *connect*, when their beings intersect as closely as two bodies during intercourse, something is poured out of one and into the other that has the power to heal the soul of its deepest wounds and restore its health. The one who receives experiences the joy of being healed. The one who gives knows the even greater joy of being used to heal. Something good is in the heart of each of God's children that is more powerful than everything bad. It's there, waiting to be released, to work its magic. But it rarely happens.[4]

4. Crabb, *Connecting*, xi.

The rarity of such connections is related to another rarity in today's busy culture, which is the cultivation of true friendship. I see this still under the heading of the church, but I want to legitimize spiritual friendship as a crucial dynamic for spiritual growth, and for healing when losses come, and something that is deeply grieved when lost.

Healing through Friendship in the Church

In her book *Grief*, Melissa Kelley catches the spirit of our vulnerability to grief because of our relational nature when she argues that "grief is a profoundly relational experience."[5] Further, she argues that since we are relational beings and vulnerable to grief, supportive relationships are critical to the healing and restoration of the bereaved. This I see to be generally true. However, it becomes emphatically true in the case of spiritual friendships. I want to illustrate the nature of these friendships in the life of a sixteenth-century nun.

Anne-Marie Ellithorpe recently has written a paper on "Teresa of Avila and Authentic Friendship,"[6] which highlights the importance of friendship in formation, healing, and transformation. Teresa was the founder of the Discalced Carmelite Order[7] and was named, in 1970, the first female Doctor of the Church. Ellithorpe notes that for Teresa, "Friendship with God is intertwined with friendship with others. Teresa advocates for communities of friendship in which friendship with God is fostered, within which all must be friends, irrespective of social status."[8] The friendship with God we have encouraged in a previous chapter "was central to Teresa's vision. The relationship with God that Teresa advocates for is an intimate friendship, in which the friends frequently spend time alone together and share the same will."[9] Teresa's encouragement of friendship ran counter to

5. Kelley, *Grief*, 126.

6. See Ellithorpe, "Teresa of Avila and Authentic Friendship."

7. Teresa wrote four books: *The Book of Her Life*, *Foundations* (finished circa 1581), *Meditations on the Song of Songs* (1566), and *The Interior Castle* (1577). She also wrote the Constitutions for the Reformed Carmelite Order (1563) a variety of smaller works, and many letters.

8. Ellithorpe, "Teresa of Avila and Authentic Friendship," 6.

9. Ibid., 5. She cites Teresa at this point: "And if one perseveres, I trust then in the mercy of God, who never fails to repay anyone who has taken Him for a friend. For mental prayer in my opinion is nothing else than an intimate sharing between friends; it means taking time frequently to be alone with Him who we know loves us. In order that love be true and the friendship endure, the wills of the friends must be in accord." Teresa,

the culture of the Spain in which she lived, where friendship could only be had within the same class and societal status. To make her point, Teresa pointed to the friendship of God with humans. Ellithorpe states,

> The fundamental answer to this, summarized from Teresa's work by Rowan Williams, is that through the Holy Spirit we are adopted into the relation of God to God. The Father treats us as deserving of the same loving respect that is due to the Son. But, Williams continues, the method of adoption further radicalizes the idea of friendship. It is not that God brings us up to an acceptable standard and then deigns to treat us as friends. Rather, in order to make us friends, God completely abandons dignity and status.[10]

Through the incarnation, the Son identifies with suffering men and women and "renounces all claim to special status."[11]

However, such friendship with God needed to be evidenced in friendship with human friends in Christ, those who shared a friendship with God, and as Ellithorpe states, "To join one of Teresa's communities was to commit oneself to friendship, to equality, and to *reciprocal pastoral care*, including both nurture and criticism."[12] This mutual pastoral care was related to the fact that "Teresa considered that the goal of true friendship with other people was *to support the friend in the life of prayer*."[13] The kind of friends Teresa has in mind are those "with whom one could share spiritual experiences," those who "want the best for one another, and the best that anyone could possibly attain would be friendship with Christ."[14] In other words, friends who help us to live the life of prayer, who help us to love Christ better and do not usurp his place in our lives.

I cannot overemphasize the importance of friendship in my life in general, and particularly during the days of crisis when my wife was diagnosed with cancer, on into the treatments, the days of hope and remission, on through the difficult season in palliative care, and into the days of acute

---

Book of Her Life, 8.5, 96.

10. Ibid., 103, 133–40; Rowan Williams, *Teresa of Avila*, 103.

11. Ellithorpe, "Teresa of Avila and Authentic Friendship," 6., Emphasis mine.

12. Ibid., Emphasis mine.

13. Ibid., 4. Emphasis mine. She cites Teresa: "Thus, daughters, in reference to all the persons who speak with you, if they are disposed and there is some friendship, try to remove any fear they may have of beginning to use so great a good. And for the love of God I beg you that your conversation always be directed toward bringing some good to the one with whom you are speaking, for your prayer must be for the benefit of souls." Teresa, *The Way of Perfection*, 20.3, 115.

14. Ibid., 8.

grieving. General human community is a common grace given to all humans. Whether or not they are noetically in Christ, all humans are related by means of their creation by God and by the incarnation of his Son into humanity, and by means of the fact that he died to reconcile all humans of every race, color, and creed to himself. When Christians demonstrate reconciliation and oneness of community in the church despite great social or racial diversity, and when Christians take a lead in expressing human community and compassion, including reconciliation and peace initiatives, they are simply taking seriously God's intended destiny for humanity in Christ.

I saw evidences everywhere of the communal image of God in the human beings who cared for Sharon, some who were persons of faith, and some not. Meeting a Scottish surgeon who happened to come to our local hospital the day of her diagnosis—a doctor who had worked in the same hospital Sharon had nursed in—brought a human connection that gave comfort to Sharon, and therefore to me. It was not only knowing she was in competent hands (you don't have to be Scottish to be competent, but it helps!), but there are certain spoken nuances and figures of speech that Scottish people "get," as well as unsaid understandings, that brought a certain comfort. This man even phoned Sharon on her palliative care bed when he knew she wasn't going to make it. That was extremely meaningful to her and to me. Then there was the care of a wonderful Irish doctor (the Irish are a close second!), a person of faith and wisdom, who supervised Sharon's chemotherapeutic care and made the effort to come to her memorial. There was a remarkable general practitioner, a close friend, who cared for Sharon in a way that I can only say was above and beyond the call of duty. He cared for me afterwards in many ways, mostly through what male friends often enjoy—side-by-side rather than face-to-face companionship, in sports and bantering and put-downs to prevent any swollen-headedness or, in the case of grieving, any self-pity. And there were other doctors and nurses in the home and in the palliative care unit and at Peace Arch, whose high-touch care was evidence of the warmth of the human community God created, and which fallenness has not totally obliterated.

But closer friendships were also crucial in the comfort Sharon experienced. Close female friends could give practical care where I was limited, and with them she could share things about her kids and her husband. The time we invest in friendships is never wasted, not for the day of grieving and storms, and not for eternity. Henri Nouwen expresses "The Gift of Friendship" in a remarkably insightful way:

> Friendship is one of the greatest gifts a human being can receive. It is a bond beyond common goals, common interests, or common histories. It is a bond stronger than sexual union can create, deeper than a shared fate can solidify, and even more intimate than the bonds of marriage or community. Friendship is being with the other in joy and sorrow, even when we cannot increase the joy or decrease the sorrow. It is a unity of souls that gives nobility and sincerity to love. Friendship makes all of life shine brightly Blessed are those who lay down their lives for their friends.[15]

Friends of the Teresa variety have been less numerous in my life, but there have been some important ones, many of whom are mentioned in the acknowledgements. When, after three years I had fallen in love again and married Tammy, I became concerned about what this might mean when I got to heaven. I worried about the mystery of how one might relate to the two people to whom one had been married . . . even knowing, of course, that there is no marriage there. My colleague Hans Boersma said something like, "Ross, life in heaven transcends all that. Marriage is just a sacrament of something much higher there." My Aussie colleague Rikk Watts said something much different—something like, "Mate, you're thinking far too possessively!" Each was helpful in his own way.

This reality of the communing presence of the "church triumphant" often comforts me, especially as I think about loved ones who have gone before. It is reflected in some great hymns of the faith, including Samuel John Stone's hymn of the 1860s, one of twelve that he based on the twelve articles of the Apostles' Creed (he called them the *Lyra Fidelium*). "The Church's One Foundation" is based on the ninth article: the holy catholic church; the communion of saints. This hymn makes the connection between the sweet communion of the church on earth with the inner life of the Trinity, and with the saints who have gone ahead:

> Yet she on earth hath union With God the Three in One,
> And mystic sweet communion With those whose rest is won,
> With all her sons and daughters, Who, by the Master's Hand
> Led through the deathly waters, Repose in Eden land.
>
> O happy ones and holy! Lord, give us grace that we
> Like them, the meek and lowly, On high may dwell with Thee . . . .[16]

---

15. Nouwen, *Bread for the Journey*, January 7.

16. There is an autographed copy in the Church Club of New York, which was written

Charles Wesley's funeral hymn, written in 1759, expresses similar sentiments not heard often in contemporary worship, which move us to faithfulness in light of those who have passed on:

> Let saints on earth in concert sing
> With those whose work is done;
> For all the servants of our king
> In Heav'n and earth are one.
>
> One family, we dwell in Him,
> One Church, above, beneath;
> Though now divided by the stream,
> The narrow stream of death.
>
> One army of the living God,
> To His command we bow;
> Part of the host have crossed the flood,
> And part are crossing now . . . .

chapter 12

Moving towards Adaptation—

GRIEF SHARING WITH THE *PEOPLE* OF THE TRIUNE GOD (2)

Care through Pastors of the Church

THE WAY IN WHICH unity and particularity, nearness and differentiation are held together in the Trinity may be an important dynamic in the pastoral care of God's people. Such a profound analogy is justified by the reality that humanity is made in God's image and that human persons are invited to participate in Christ, in the life of God. God, who has revealed himself in the person and work of his Son by the person and work of the Holy Spirit, is the one God, one in essence and one in communion. But he is at the same time the one God in three persons—each of whom, though equal in essence and honor, has irreducible identity. They are differentiated at minimum by their relations to each other. The Father is not the Son, and the Spirit is not the Father. Each is in the other in a mutuality of perfect communion (Jesus said, "I am in my Father and my Father is in me"), yet each is given space to be who each is (for example, it is the Son who alone becomes incarnate and dies on the cross). In other words, there is a nearness or intimacy of the persons and *at the same time*, a distinctness or differentiation of each person. Each is given space to be. What would be the point of Jesus' prayer at Gethsemane, *"Father, if you are willing, take this cup from me; yet not my will, but yours be done"* (Luke 22:42), unless the Son of God was a differentiated person, with space in which to think and feel and will?

Neil Pembroke finds this spatial dynamic within the Trinity ("contrast without conflict") an important foundation for pastoral care and counseling.[1] He argues that "effective pastoral counseling involves both moving in close through empathy and acceptance, and creating appropriate distance through a process that Martin Buber refers to as confirmation."[2] More precisely, Pembroke states that "effective pastoral caregivers know when and how to move in close, and when and how to create appropriate distance." He surmises that "A very important pastoral art . . . is managing the interpersonal space."[3] Drawing near is facilitated through empathy and acceptance; moving out facilitates confrontation.

Another way of viewing this, as Pembroke does, is to employ a concept named by David Cunningham in his reflection on the triune nature of God. He uses the language of *polyphony* to describe the coinherence of oneness and threeness within the Trinity. This technical musical term refers to "simultaneous, non-excluding difference: that is, more than one note is played at a time, and none of these notes is so dominant that it renders another mute."[4] Thus Cunningham makes the observation that "a theological perspective informed by polyphony would challenge any view that claims that any two contrastive categories must necessarily work against each other."[5] The "zero-sum game" is to be avoided in favor of thinking "in terms of simultaneous difference that need not be synthesized into a single, homogeneous unity."[6] The humanity and deity of the one person, Jesus Christ, and the transcendence and immanence of God, are good examples. In applying this concept to the doctrine of the Trinity, Pembroke states that the "fundamental polyphonic categories are unity and difference."[7]

I find myself in complete harmony with Pembroke's application of Cappadocian theology of the Trinity in pastoral care,[8] employing the image-of-God theological anthropology of Colin Gunton. Pembroke expresses agreement with the belief that the *telos* of pastoral care is "helping people to grow into the likeness of God." Since sin tarnishes the image of God, the task of the pastor is co-managing "the inter-personal space" be-

---

1. Pembroke, "Space in the Trinity and Pastoral Care," 3.1–10.

2. Ibid., 3.1.

3. Ibid.

4. Cunningham, *These Three Are One*, 128.

5. Pembroke, "Space in the Trinity and Pastoral Care," 3.2.

6. Cunningham, *These Three Are One*, 131.

7. Pembroke, "Space in the Trinity and Pastoral Care," 3.2.

8. I am a little less accommodating (less polyphonic) than Pembroke of the Thomist Western Trinitarian viewpoint, which speaks of persons *as* relations.

tween the pastor and the person being cared for, so that the grace of Christ can restore persons and conform them to the likeness of God. At a practical level, this involves "attending to certain psychological, spiritual, and moral issues" towards that *telos*. Pembroke employs Gunton's relational ontology, which uses space to guide it. In applying this, Pembroke asserts that space must be properly defined and managed: "If there is too much space in the relational sphere there is a fall into individualism. Mutual participation in relationship implies nearness. Too little space, on the other hand, is also a problem. When the other sits on top of me, so to speak, I lose my freedom. She fails to make room for me and so shows a lack of respect for my otherness."[9] These extremely valuable but somewhat intuitive notions concerning relational space are justified, in Gunton's understanding, by way of analogy with the Trinity:

> We have a conception of *personal space*: the space in which three persons are for and from each other in their otherness. They thus confer particularity upon and receive it from one another. That giving of particularity is very important: it is a matter of space to be. Father, Son and Spirit through the shape—the *taxis*—of their inseparable relatedness confer particularity and freedom on each other. That is their personal being.[10]

Drawing on this, Pembroke concludes that if God is persons-in-communion, and humanity is made in his image, then a crucial dynamic of that image is our relationality, and our mutual participation in one another's lives will define our humanity. We "will experience our humanity in our relatedness to others . . ." and "[t]he structure or *taxis* of human community is a relationality that involves both participation (nearness) and otherness (distance)."[11] Otherness and relation become the polarity that is polyphony. As Gunton states, "To be a person is to be constituted in particularity and freedom—to be given space to be—by others in community. . . . Only where both are given due stress is personhood fully enabled."[12]

It is not difficult to surmise where the argument now travels with respect to the care of a pastor, or for any two Christians caring for one another. The *telos* of pastoral care is for persons to be in relation in a way that is polyphonic—persons validating one another in a communion that is

9. Pembroke, "Space in the Trinity and Pastoral Care," 3.3.

10. Gunton, *Promise of Trinitarian Theology*, 113. Emphasis added.

11. Pembroke, "Space in the Trinity and Pastoral Care," 3.3.

12. Gunton, *Promise of Trinitarian Theology*, 117.

mutually intimate and affirming. The pastor will always be on the journey of bringing her/his being as a healthy person-in-relation into communion with the other, avoiding nearness that squashes the other while avoiding aloofness and distance that denies the existence of the other. Pembroke develops this pastoral rubric by expanding on the themes of *nearness* and *distance* in pastoral care and counseling. My own preference is for the term *differentiation* (over *distance*), though I understand that in this case, "distance" is intended to convey something positive—the giving of space that avoids enmeshment.

Nearness in Pastoral Care and Counseling

Managing the space within a pastoral relationship is "expressed first and foremost through empathic attunement,"[13] says Pembroke. He cites Egan, who speaks of empathy as "an attempt to penetrate the metaphysical aloneness of the other."[14] Pembroke elaborates, stating that "Empathy involves an attempt to put oneself in contact. It is an antidote to psychic loneliness. When a person receives an empathic response, she is no longer alone in her pain and confusion; she has a friend to share it with."[15] Pembroke stresses that empathy is what keeps pastors or therapists from looking at parishioners or clients as specimens to be studied in an aloof manner. Caregivers need to go into the world of the person being cared for, to "sense from the inside what life is like for her."[16] He makes reference to Carl Rogers's definition of empathy, which has an "as if" reality to it, while preserving the personhood of the pastor intact:

> To sense the client's private world as if it were your own, but without ever losing the "as if" quality—this is empathy, and this seems essential to therapy. To sense the client's anger, fear, or confusion as if it were your own, yet without your own anger, fear, or confusion getting bound up with it, is the condition we are endeavouring to describe.[17]

---

13. Pembroke, "Space in the Trinity and Pastoral Care," 3.4.

14. Egan, *Skilled Helper*, 123.

15. Pembroke, "Space in the Trinity and Pastoral Care," 3.4.

16. Ibid.

17. Rogers, "Necessary and sufficient conditions," 226.

In other words: even in nearness, differentiation must be preserved in a healthy helping relationship.

When a pastor, or indeed any Christian, cares for another person, an even more important dynamic is at work than merely exemplifying the polyphony of the Trinity with respect to nearness and intact, irreducible identity. The pastor is first in a participational relationship with the Trinity; s/he is in Christ, and Christ is by the Spirit in her or him. Indeed, the person being cared for or counseled, if a Christian, is also in that relationship to Christ. Something is shared between one and the other that unites them, and that in-ness of each with God can become the means for an interaction that brings healing and growth. This dynamic is all too infrequently pressed into in the life of the church. Our relationship with the living God and with one another is often shallow, and the new covenant dynamics therefore may not operate.

It is interesting to note that when Paul wishes to motivate and impart strength for the growth of the people of God at Corinth, he begins an important paragraph on that theme with these words: *"As God's co-workers we urge you not to receive God's grace in vain"* (2 Cor 6:1). Paul is completely aware that any hope of his presence bringing comfort and inspiring growth in the people of God is a function of his co-working with God, his participation in Christ by the Spirit. Pastors can only bring a comforting presence to bereaved people to the extent that they mediate the presence of Christ; that is, as they live into their "in-ness" in Christ by the Spirit.

Even Jesus, in his public ministry, brought comfort to the broken as a consequence of lived communion with the Father, by the Spirit (Luke 4:14–19). His life is lived in the polyphony of communion with the Father by the Spirit. What Jesus did and all that he said flowed from his in-ness with the Father. He said, *"Very truly I tell you, the Son can do nothing by himself; he can do only what he sees his Father doing, because whatever the Father does the Son also does"* (John 5:19). But this revelation of the Son's perichoretic relationship with the Father, issuing in his words and deeds in John 5, anticipates *"greater works"* (John 5:20) that Jesus would do—and, crucially, what his people would do also—by the Spirit (John 14:12 *"they will do even greater things than these, because I am going to the Father"*). The heart of the Christian gospel is that believing people are brought into union with Christ by the Spirit. They participate in the very life of God, and so they can minister to one another and a broken world, confident that as they live in communion with God, his words will become their words, bringing comfort to the broken.

But of course, this *union* does not imply that we do not have to engage actively in *communion* with the living God. Spiritual practices are analogous to what it takes to have a good marriage. The union established by a marriage only facilitates the pursuit of communion. Too many pastors in the North American church have allowed their lives to be swamped with busyness that often shores up a poor self worth. Spiritual practices in the life of the pastor are crucial to the effectiveness of our "presence" and the things we say as we discern the movements of the soul in those we care for. One text that anticipated this prophetically in Jesus, a text I have made central in my own pastoral ministry, is Isaiah 50:4: *"The Sovereign Lord has given me a well-instructed tongue, to know the word that sustains the weary. He wakens me morning by morning, wakens my ear to listen like one being instructed."* The essence of pastoral care for the grieving and all other needs is a *"well-instructed tongue,"* one that is informed by a listening ear and a submissive heart, attuned to the voice of the Father by means of "morning by morning" communion and contemplation. This practiced communion will be crucial in the second aspect of pastoral care—that of differentiation and confirmation.

Distance (Differentiation) in Pastoral Care and Counseling

Pembroke states that "one crucial expression of distance is a willingness to go beyond empathy in order to challenge or confront the other person."[18] He speaks of this kind of confrontation as necessary on occasion "to help a person move toward psychological, moral and spiritual maturity." Pembroke pits Martin Buber's concept of *confirmation* of the person over against Rogers's notion of *acceptance*. Buber thought that beyond the unconditional regard for what the person is ("I take you as you are"), there is the seeing of potential; that is, the need to act with the other towards what the person can be. Buber stated, "And now I not only accept the other as he is, but I confirm him, in myself, and then in him, in relation to this potentiality that is meant by him and it can now be developed. . . . He can do more or less to this scope but I can, too, do something."[19] In other words, "imaging the potential of the other and actively helping in realization of

18. Pembroke, "Space in the Trinity and Pastoral Care," 3.4.
19. Buber, *Knowledge of Man*, 182.

that potential constitute for Buber the critical points of distinction between acceptance and confirmation."[20]

In sum, Rogers insisted on unconditional positive regard as the strongest factor in promoting change, while Buber valued confirmation over acceptance. Buber also recognized the polar reality of human beings. For him, the poles were not "good and evil" so much as "yes and no." Buber still thought that even this act of confirming preserved space for the person, who remained very much intact as a person. Buber described the process as an "unfolding" in which he would "struggle with the other against herself not to impose a direction, but to facilitate a release of that which was latent in her." Buber's viewpoint fits well a biblical anthropology that takes into account both the fact that humans are created in the image of God *and* that because of the fall they are innately sinful. The polarity spoken of by Buber could have been heard from the apostle Paul when he speaks of the yes and no with such passion in Romans 7. The gospel of Christ declares the great "Yes" and empowers Christian disciples against the "No"s . . . but discipleship and pastoral care are still needed, for the Yes often grows dim, while the No to holiness so easily awakens in this age when the kingdom has come, yet not fully.

Providing care for someone grieving in the initial stages is primarily about empathy. However, in the nearness that is involved in empathy, the pastor will need to both foster communion and maintain his/her differentiation. For some persons in the acute phase of grieving, who are unable to feel much due to the anaesthetic of shock (or a host of other reasons), confirmation (per Buber) may be necessary after a while. The encouraged "yes" will be giving permission to grieve. For some it will be a "be gentle with yourself" exhortation, especially when the determination to move on is superficial and a result of denial.

My anecdotal experience in pastoral ministry is that persons (especially men) who marry quickly after the loss of their spouse frequently end up in deeply conflicted marriages. Confirmation, to use the term in Buber's way, may mean asking widowed persons to say no to a premature betrothal or sexual urges that mask the grief, pain, and anger they have still to process. There is no rule for when a person should remarry, but a rule of thumb suggests a one-year minimum, and two if there are teen or young adult children involved. Grief can place a veil over one's eyes in evaluating future potential spouses, and feelings of deep grief for a deceased loved one can be

20. Pembroke, "Space in the Trinity and Pastoral Care," 3.4.

redirected into powerful urges of a romantic nature. Keeping the counsel of trusted friends and pastors is important in such a vulnerable season.

Expanding on this, a pastor's most significant contributions in the journey of loss and grieving are fourfold: the offering of empathic *presence* before and after the loss, in the season of acute grief, and then secondly, when the appropriate time comes, offering *perspective* on what God is saying and doing in the midst of this soul journey or pilgrimage. This may involve confirmation. A third contribution would be to offer skills of discernment and a well-chosen *referral* to a medical doctor or professional counselor, if the grief is complicated and depression ensues (see the following chapter). For a pastor to know her/his limitations is all-important. Fourthly—although often earlier in chronological order—is to gently guide the family through burial or cremation, and through a *memorial* service, and to encourage communal and family rituals that help with the process of grief.

Let me elaborate on all four contributions.

Firstly, the matter of *presence* is vitally important. Pastors often worry—when they are called to visit a spouse or family in the vigil awaiting a loved one's passing, or who have just received a diagnosis, or have just learned of a loved one's death—about whether they will be able to find choice words to say. In fact, it is the non-anxious presence of a pastor that ministers most effectively. This mirrors the presence of Jesus with these grieving people—his presence at their side, and his presence at the right hand of the Father praying for them. The memory will live with me to my dying day of the Sunday evening when my wife and I were called to the home of some friends in our church. Their son, a pilot, had just gone down in an aircraft over Vancouver Island near Nanaimo. The father and mother and fiancée were there, as well as some friends who had lost their daughter a few years before. They did not yet know for sure that he was dead, and they awaited word from the authorities investigating the crash. We waited with them for around three hours, until the phone rang and the call confirmed that he had died.

What did we do for three hours? Offer false hope? Make polite and inane conversation? Read Scripture? We may have done some of the latter, and I hesitate to say that we did things "right." Rather, I think they just appreciated that we were *there. Present* to them. Attentive to them, not to our performance. Offering hugs and cups of tea. And of course, when the moment came, to offer more hugs and to hold them and when time seemed appropriate, to pray with them. To hear their anguish and anger, and watch for signs of shock. To follow up over the next few days, and to work with them towards a burial and an honoring memorial service.

There are, of course, things to say and not to say, at particular times. For example, offering a guess about the everlasting destiny of a person is probably never appropriate, given that none of us knows the human heart but God. For children who die before the "age of responsibility," it is my considered opinion that in light of what Jesus said about children being the very essence of the kingdom of God, they are taken into God's presence when they die. That does not mean I have no doctrine of original sin. It simply means that Christ has, by virtue of his vicarious life and atoning death, taken away the guilt and sin of humanity, and it simply means that children—who by their very disposition reflect faith—are justified and redeemed. From this theology, I can offer comfort to parents in what is possibly the greatest loss of all. But if that is not the theological position of a pastor, there may be times when it is important for that pastor to share that . . . but I can't think when! Certainly not in the crisis moments of loss. And refusing to offer a memorial service to a family in light of gospel hope, in the midst of such grief, is unthinkable.

An attentive pastor who is present with loved ones throughout the vigil of a dying person will have a watchful eye over the loved ones for discerning between stoical rather than Christian ways of being—that is, avoidance of reality in the name of being "strong"—and encourage them gently to face reality and pray with them for comfort. Also, Christians who believe in contemporary divine healing tend to use their "faith" to avoid facing the possibility that their loved ones are dying. The danger is that when the loved one does die, no grieving—either by the dying person as he or she died, or by the persons who remain—has occurred. I am a believer in God's ability to heal, and that the kingdom of God has come, and with it, healings do happen. I pray for people who are dying to be healed; I have been so bold, when the seven-year-old son of a single mother died, as to pray for a resurrection. But this theology of healing must be balanced with two other realities: the fact that the kingdom has not yet *fully* come, and the fact that until Jesus comes again, we need a theology of suffering as well as healing. The theology of glory must be tempered with the theology of suffering in this in-between time of the kingdom. Glory and all healing and resurrection is for the day when Christ returns. When God in his mercy and power does heal someone, this is meant to be an encouragement for all, including those who have not been healed, that Christ is indeed alive and that resurrection is going to be a reality for all! Prayers for healing with genuine faith must be offered in submission to the will of the Father, and therefore, two things will be held in tension all the way up to the moment of death: God may heal, but he may not. In light of the latter possibility, one needs to prepare for a loved one's possible death and to say the kind of things that need to be said for good closure.

The pastor's presence, if desired, can be a huge comfort in the moments of the passing. Sometimes people desire the utmost privacy, and that must be respected. The pastor can offer some insights about the nature of acute grief and shock, if that seems appropriate. Ensuring people have friends to support them will be crucial.

When desired again, and mourners seek the *perspective* of a pastor as grief develops, the pastor should focus primarily on bringing people into the presence of God, making them aware that the Lord Jesus gathers up all their grief and brings intercession to the Father—and comfort to them, by the Spirit. The pastor will be attentive to the movements of the mourners' souls and encourage them to experience their emotions. When they are ready, introduce them to reading the Psalms as a way to pray and to experience their loss, grief, anger, and so on.

When the time comes and the mourner is ready, offer guidance regarding spiritual practices. Confirmation that results from being in the wrestling process on a number of possible issues may be required. As Friedman suggests, this entering into another's wrestling is not permission for me "to impose myself on you and say, 'I know better than you.' It is only insofar as you share with me and as we struggle together that I can glimpse the person you are called to become."[21] If it is evident that the grief process is complicated and the mourner is stuck, a *referral* may be necessary; a pastor should cultivate relationships with some doctors, psychiatrists, and psychotherapists in the community to gain a sense of mutual confidence in them. It can be crucial to the nature of the church as a body, and as a priesthood in which all are priests, that the pastor is not the only person who cares for grieving people. Recognizing and equipping other persons with pastoral and wisdom giftings in a congregation is important. These gifted persons, who have often gone through loss themselves, are able to offer a certain level of care for grieving people. Stephen Ministries is one form this can take. Many congregations offer the Griefshare program, which

---

21. Friedman, "Reflections on the Buber-Rogers Debate," 63–64.

can also facilitate caring. In any of these programs, it will be important for participants to have pastoral support and to know their own limitations.

Guiding mourners through a burial or cremation and memorial service requires great sensitivity to culture and other realities. Developing relationships with funeral directors and staff will help pastors give guidance to the family on what is involved in having the body taken to the funeral home and what is involved in either burial or cremation.[22] Planning the memorial service is also a skillful dance between encouraging full family participation and the pastor's own wise guidance. As for the overall tone, some families opt for a "celebration of life"; this can be done to an extreme that does not permit the expression of lament and feels like denial. There is such a thing as defiant joy, and it is not the same as denial. I have seen joy in the face of reality. Yet other services are so doleful that resurrection hope seems remote. Reading the emotional state of the mourners and the congregation will allow the pastor to reflect a sensitive response. Here are some practical notes from many years of conducting memorial services:

(i) Preach for a short time—fifteen minutes at most.

(ii) Try to have the sermon earlier rather than later in the service, because eulogies can take a long time, so that no one might be listening when homily time arrives. I have almost always found that when I am asked to speak at a memorial service, the Holy Spirit implants a passage in my mind. If this doesn't happen, or in concert with this, I may ask if the deceased had any favorite passages of Scripture, or if there was a theme about his or her life that could be amplified from a scriptural text. I once conducted a memorial for a bus driver known well in Victoria, British Columbia. Everyone spoke of his friendliness, so I spoke to a large group, most of whom were not people of faith, on friendship. My homily referred to the man and pointed beyond him to Jesus as the friend of sinners, the friend who sticks closer than a brother.

---

22. Pastors, if asked, may, of course, offer an opinion on which of these options they prefer. This should be done with appropriate humility and with a clear understanding that this is not a clearly revealed matter, from a biblical perspective. The covenant people of God throughout the Scriptures showed great reverence for the dead human body, and burial is their preferred method, as it was for our Lord. But these arguments are from precedence, not principle. Environmental and financial concerns are legitimate factors in our day. No one should be made to feel that cremation is secondary. We all know that the miracle of resurrection when it comes will be a miracle no matter where the remains of a person might be!

(iii) Ask for family input for the hymns and worship songs, as they will offer choices that were meaningful to the deceased or the family. Music
has an enormous evoking and comforting effect.

(iv) Include a significant amount of Scripture reading, depending on the
nature of the congregation; liturgical churches will have meaningful
liturgies that frame and inform the service and facilitate communion
with the saints of the past.

A much-neglected aspect of the cure of grieving souls in Western
contemporary culture is that of communal rituals. These rituals acknowledge the embodied and communal nature of our personhood and the way
we grieve and move on. Jewish people, for example, learned as an ancient
society what it means to experience loss, and they formed rituals for experiencing grief—including the tradition of *shiva* for seven days following the
death.

> During *shiva*, one does not work, bathe, put on shoes, engage in
> intercourse, read Torah or have one's hair cut. The mourners are to
> behave as though they themselves had died. The first response to
> death is to give inconsolable grief its due. Such grief is assimilated
> during the seven days of *shiva*, and then tempered by a month of
> more moderate mourning. After a year all mourning is set aside,
> except for the praying of *Kaddish*, the prayer for the dead, on the
> anniversary of the death.[23]

As Richard Neuhaus wisely states, "Traditions of wisdom encourage
us to stay with death a while."[24] There is a kind of modern emotivism that
says emotional authenticity is everything, and all that matters is authentic feeling. On this viewpoint "mere ritual" is considered suspect, maybe
even artificial and dishonest. However, we are embodied persons within
creation, not spirits seeking to escape from creation. Rituals of an earthy
and communal kind bring healing, sometimes in ways that go beyond what
we feel at the time.

Care through Counselors

The importance of community in healing cannot be overemphasized. I
consider good counseling, including grief counseling, to be very much part

23. Neuhaus, *Eternal Pity*, 4.
24. Ibid.

of human community. In the case of Christian counselors, their work is an expression of the giftedness and wisdom of a person in a church community. Counselors are people with wisdom and training, and they can be important in the healing journey, especially for those with complicated grief. Ruth Davis Konigsberg has written a celebrated article in which she summarizes recent thinking about grief in the field of psychology and psychotherapy. She explodes some popular myths about the grief process and evaluates the need for counseling for people with "normal" grief responses.[25] Here are some of her findings:

i.   The stages of grief as proposed by Kübler-Ross are increasingly viewed with skepticism in academia, though "they still hold sway with practitioners and the general public."[26]

ii. Expressing negative emotions does not necessarily have a healing effect and can actually prolong distress. In a 2007 study of sixty-six people who had recently lost a spouse or child, those who did not express their negative emotions six months after their loss were less depressed and anxious and had fewer health complaints at fourteen and twenty-five months than those who did express negative emotions. The study, which included a control group of non-bereaved participants and which was conducted by George Bonanno, a professor at Columbia University's Teachers College specializing in the psychology of loss and trauma, suggests that tamping down or avoiding those feelings, known as "repressive coping," actually has a protective function.

iii. The "grief work hypothesis," which defines grief as a project that must be tackled in order to prevent psychological problems, was also viewed to be a myth. This notion—which came from Freud, who spoke of the "work of mourning"—had become the guiding metaphor for modern grief theory. But Konigsberg notes that "a 60-person study conducted by the husband-and-wife research team Wolfgang and Margaret Stroebe[27] of Utrecht University found that widows who avoided confronting their loss were not any more depressed than widows who 'worked through' their grief. As to the importance of giving grief a

25. Konigsberg, "New Ways to Think about Grief," 1–4.

26. All quotations in this section, unless otherwise specified, are from Konigsberg, "New Ways to Think about Grief," 1–2.

27. See Stroebe et al., *Handbook of Bereavement Research and Practice.*

voice, several other studies done by the Stroebes indicated that talking or writing about the death of a spouse did not help people adjust to that loss any better."[28]

iv. While it is acknowledged that loss lasts forever, acute grief usually has a duration of about six months. A personal note here: whereas this seems to be based on how soon people begin to "function normally" after this period, I believe that using this figure as a guideline for re-entering a relationship and marriage is unwise. In my experience as a pastor counseling others, I would have to say that, as already mentioned, most people should wait at least a year, and if one has children, two years is minimal, for all kinds of reasons.

v. The only instance in which counseling showed a benefit was when it was targeted at people displaying marked difficulties adapting to loss. One researcher, Currier, referring to the statistical norm for grief's length and intensity, notes that "Given the current research, we cannot say that grief counseling is as effective with adults who are showing a normative response."[29]

Konigsberg concludes:

> Instead of rushing to prescribe ways to grieve, it would be more helpful to spread a different, more liberating message based on what the science is beginning to tell us: that most people are re-silient enough to get through loss on their own without stages or phases or tasks. A small minority will have a much harder time of it, and clinicians should focus their efforts on tailoring interventions for this group that are based on evidence, not assumptions.[30]

George Bonanno's work on grief, to which Konigsberg refers, also challenges the one-size-fits-all approach to evaluating the ways in which people grieve.[31] Crying, which is considered to be a normal part of grieving for many people, is not the only healthy response and may even be harmful if forced or excessive. Other responses, which Bonanno calls "coping ugly,"

28. Konigsberg, "New Ways to Think about Grief," 2.

29. Currier, Neimeyer and Berman, "The Effectiveness of Psychotherapeutic Interventions for the Bereaved: A Comprehensive Quantitative Review," 648–61, cited in Konigsberg, "New Ways to Think about Grief," 4.

30. Konigsberg, "New Ways to Think about Grief," 4.

31. See Bonanno, "Loss, Trauma, and Human Resilience," 20–28. See also Bonanno et al., "Resilience to Loss and Chronic Grief," 1150–64.

may appear to be counterintuitive or even dysfunctional ways of resolving grief. These include celebratory responses, laughter, or self-serving bias in interpreting events. Lack of crying or talking it out, Bonanno suggests, may in fact be a sign of resilience.[32] Bonanno's work has been a major influence challenging the stage theory approach of Kübler-Ross (denial, anger, bargaining, depression, acceptance)—a theme Konigsberg also challenged, as we have noted. Bonanno's large body of peer-reviewed studies on large numbers of grieving people has thus demonstrated that many people do not grieve "normally," but are "resilient."[33]

However, it must be pointed out that Currier et al., among others, have challenged Bonanno. They write that "Although people tend to respond to bereavement in a resilient manner or regain pre-loss levels of functioning after a protracted period of distress (Bonanno et al., 2002), research has also documented that the nature of an individual's grief response can increase the risk for serious decrements in mental and physical health (see Prigerson, Vanderwerker, & Maciejewski, 2008 for review)."[34]

Bonanno's approach, in my opinion, seems to proffer the virtues of Stoicism. This has some merit, but it is not grounded in a biblical anthropology, and specifically the biblical (Judeo-Christian) approach to emotional honesty as the road to healing. Much child-rearing in Western society, and especially the rearing of sons, exerts pressure towards emotional stoicism, as if this were a virtue. It's not that bravery is a bad thing, nor that rearing whimpering crybabies is a good thing. Rather, the biblical way of dealing with emotion—if the Psalms are any guideline—is to encourage the experiencing of emotion and then to exert wisdom with respect to its expression.

Not to cry was the felt ethos of my experience of departure for boarding school, or what little I can remember of those bleak occasions at train stations. You don't cry because this is the work of the Lord your parents are doing. You don't cry at the train station because boys are strong and they don't shame their parents by crying or bawling or holding on to them as the train departs. You follow the rest of the children in an orderly way into the

---

32. See also Stix, "Neuroscience of True Grit," 28–33.

33. Bonanno et al., "Resilience to Loss and Chronic Grief," 1150–64.

34. See Currier et al., "Bereavement, Religion, and Posttraumatic Growth," 69–77. See also Larson, "Taking Stock," 349–52, which is a helpful review of Doka and Tucci, *Beyond Kübler-Ross*. "Prigerson, Vanderwerker, & Maciejewski, 2008" refers to H. G. Prigerson, L. C. Vanderwerker, and P. K. Maciejewski, "A Case for Inclusion of Prolonged Grief Disorder in DSM-V," in Stroebe et al. (eds.), *Handbook of Bereavement Research and Practice*, 165–86.

train and keep up a fake smile, and wave good-bye in a formal fashion. This was the stoic way. A more biblical way (besides not sending young children away!) would have been for a father and a son to have a chat about how difficult this was going to be, for a father and mother to have expressed their own sadness, and to encourage a son to feel his own sadness, to give space and permission for tears, if tears were forthcoming. To reassure him that the Lord was with him and knew his sadness.

In fairness also to Kübler-Ross, it must be said that knowing the stages can be useful for helping both dying patients and grieving people identify and experience their emotions, as long as the provisos are understood—that the stages are *not prescriptive, not linear, and not universal.* Thus, while stage theories have come under fire for a variety of reasons, I suspect that most academic psychologists and clinicians would agree that there are some loosely discernible phases in the process, and that knowing about these can cause a comforting normalization effect. These phases have been outlined as shock and denial, intense concern, despair and depression, and then recovery, so that the loss is accepted and the bereaved person can move on in life. Shock is "the person's emotional protection from being too suddenly overwhelmed by the loss. The person may not yet be willing or able to believe what their mind knows to be true. This stage normally lasts two to three months."[35] The "intense concern" phase is one in which the grieving person is unable to think of anything else, and conversation perpetually turns to the topic. This period often lasts for six months to a year. The "despair and depression" phase, a long one, is the most painful. The bereaved person gradually comes to terms with the reality of the loss. It involves a wide range of emotions and behaviors, some of which may be irrational. With depression come feelings of anger, guilt, sadness, and anxiety. Recovery is not the elimination of all memories or pain, but the emerging of new interest in life and the ability to function normally again. "The goal is to reorganize one's life, so the loss is an important part of life rather than its center."[36]

When does a grieving person need counseling? First, J. W. Worden makes a helpful distinction between grief counseling and grief therapy. He clarifies that "Counseling involves helping people facilitate uncomplicated or normal grief to a healthy adaptation to the tasks of mourning within a

---

35. Center, *Grief and Loss*, and Smith, "Unit 1 Live Session." Both are cited in Wikipedia, *Grief*.

36. Wikipedia, *Grief*.

reasonable time frame," whereas he reserves "the term *grief therapy* for those specialized techniques . . . that are used to help people with abnormal or complicated grief reactions."[37] Worden goes on to define four goals of grief counseling, and these may help to discern who may need such counseling. They are (1) increasing the reality of the loss, (2) helping the counselee deal with both the emotional and the behavioral loss, (3) helping the counselee overcome various impediments to readjustment after the loss, and (4) helping the counselee find a way to maintain a bond with the deceased while feeling comfortable reinvesting in life. The process will involve helping the counselee to identify and experience feelings like sadness and anger, to find some meaning in the loss and to help facilitate emotional relocation. Worden offers some excellent guidelines for this process and who is competent to counsel.[38] Signs of abnormal or complicated grief reactions[39] and appropriate therapy are also described helpfully in Worden's book.[40]

I consider receiving good counseling, if needed, to be a communal event, as stated at the start of this chapter. It can also be a spiritual practice, giving attentiveness to the movements in our souls. We turn now from church and communal practices to personal practices that can be helpful in processing our grief.

37. Worden, *Grief Counseling*, 83.

38. Ibid., 80–104. See also guidelines for group counseling, 109–17.

39. Ibid., 146–52. Usually this involves self-diagnosis of chronic grief by the counselee. Absence of grief at the time of loss, or inhibited grief, contributes to this complicated grief (155). Worden speaks of chronic, delayed, exaggerated, and masked grief as four types of complicated grieving. Though there are similarities to depression, Neimeyer and Hogan contend that complicated grief is distinct from depression (R. A. Neimeyer and N. Hogan, "Quantitative or Qualitative? Measurement Issues in the Study of Grief" in Stroebe et al. (eds.), *Handbook of Bereavement Research and Practice*, 89–118.

40. Worden, *Grief Counseling*, 153–74.

chapter 13

Moving towards Adaptation—

GRIEF SHARING WITH GOD THROUGH

PERSONAL PRACTICES . . .

ONE OF THE MOST significant sources of comfort in my loss has been the gift of spiritual practices, which are receptacles of God's grace, for participation in his triune life and love. Once again, I consider these—though we are now considering personal practices—as very much communal and ecclesial. They are framed in a communal context, and their ultimate aim is fruitfulness in community. There is definitely a time, usually the acute phase, when these practices are impossible for a grieving (or depressed) person, and they should never be used like a club to guilt and hurt people. The pastors of the Puritan era in England knew souls well enough not to urge folks who were suffering from depression to read their Bibles. Rather, they read short passages for them. However, the time comes when concentration does allow such practices. The following are three I have found helpful. Much more has been written on these by others. I simply want to share some that have been helpful in my grieving process.

The Eucharist

Attending and receiving the Lord's Supper has been, for me, one of the most comforting and healing of the ecclesial practices. It is the foremost communal act of the church. It brings a renewed awareness of the suffering of Christ for us. It is a fresh immersion into the love of God for us. Most relevantly, in our partaking of bread and wine, we feed on Christ and are, in the ascended Christ, our Great High Priest, carried up, with all our grief, into the inner life of God. Laura Smit's exposition of Calvin's teaching on the sacrament expresses this so well. With regard to Calvin's fourth point in this teaching, she asserts that "the movement of the supper is not a downward movement, of Christ being drawn to us, but an upward movement, as we are lifted to him."[1] Commenting on George Hunsinger's appellation of this idea of Calvin's as an "upward vector,"[2] Smit adds, "Whereas the doctrine of transubstantiation suggests the movement of dispersal, Calvin teaches that Christ is ascended in the body and, through the sacrament, draws all believers into union with him and thus into communion with the inner life of the Trinity, suggesting the movement of convergence."[3] Smit affirms that Calvin's perspective thus "suggests an expansion of the body of Christ." She explains this by reference to the enhypostatic movement of Christ:

> In Christ's ascension, humanity is ushered into the presence of the Godhead. Through our union with him, the body of Christ that is the Church expands, not because the physical body of Christ is distributed throughout the world, but rather because we are lifted into heaven with him. We add nothing to Jesus Christ, who is already fully God, and already fills heaven and earth in his divine nature. Instead, we are expanded, adding a heavenly dimension to our lives already now, because we are united with Christ.[4]

This, Smit adds, Calvin calls "the wonderful exchange" God has made with us:

> . . . that, becoming Son of man with us, he has made us sons of God with him; that, by his descent to earth, he has prepared an ascent to heaven for us; that, by taking on our mortality, he has conferred his immortality upon us; that, accepting our weakness, he has strengthened us by his power; that, receiving our poverty unto himself, he has transferred his wealth to us; that, taking the weight of our iniquity upon himself (which oppressed us), he has clothed us with righteousness.[5]

1. Smit, "Developing a Calvinist Sacramental Theology," 9.
2. Hunsinger, "The Bread that we Break," 251.
3. Smit, "Developing a Calvinist Sacramental Theology," 9.
4. Ibid., 10.
5. Calvin, *Institutes*, IV.xvii.2.

Smit then uses the language of participation or union to affirm that "This exchange happens particularly in the supper, because union with Christ is its fruit."[6] What we most need, as the wounded and broken and mourning people of God, is to come as often as we can to the Eucharist and to find ourselves afresh in union and communion with the sympathetic and saving Priest who is our all-sufficient Lord. Nothing comforts us, nothing forms us, and nothing transforms us like gazing on Christ in this way, week by week and year by year, until he comes.

The Attentive Reading of Scripture, Especially Lament

The kind of realism and emotional honesty that we have encouraged in this book is true to what it means to be truly human, as that is understood within the general framework of biblical anthropology. It is also reflected in the Christian Scriptures, and especially the Psalms. 40 percent of the Psalms are lament, and a steady diet of the Psalms in our daily readings can be beneficial (I have personally been greatly nourished by reading a psalm in my daily readings since age fourteen.) We commented in the Introduction on Brueggeman's speaking of lament as the formfulness of grief. The Psalms give our grieving an intellectual, theological, affective, and prayer-evoking form. One psalm that ministered deeply to me in the acute phase of my mourning was Psalm 16. It is emotionally raw and authentic, but it is much more than that. It evokes the comfort of the great God of creation and covenant in a personal "I-Thou" relationship way (vv. 1–2), demonstrated in experiential enjoyment and trust (vv. 5–7); it invokes the comfort of the community of God (v. 3), warns against distractions that can cause us to avoid the reality of grief (v. 4); and it provokes the hope of resurrection (vv. 9–11).

Psalm 16, A miktam of David.

Keep me safe, my God, for in you I take refuge.

I say to the Lord, "You are my Lord; apart from you I have no good thing."

I say of the holy people who are in the land, "They are the noble ones in whom is all my delight."

Those who run after other gods will suffer more and more. I will not pour out libations of blood to such gods or take up their names on my lips.

Lord, you alone are my portion and my cup; you make my lot secure.

6. Smit, "Developing a Calvinist Sacramental Theology," 10.

The boundary lines have fallen for me in pleasant places; surely I have a delightful inheritance.

I will praise the Lord, who counsels me; even at night my heart instructs me.

I keep my eyes always on the Lord. With him at my right hand, I will not be shaken.

Therefore my heart is glad and my tongue rejoices; my body also will rest secure,

because you will not abandon me to the realm of the dead, nor will you let your faithful one see decay.

You make known to me the path of life; you will fill me with joy in your presence,

with eternal pleasures at your right hand.

The literary or musical caption, "A *miktam* of David"—though we cannot be sure of its meaning—is only present in the superscript of Davidic prayers that express great danger and threat of loss (see Psalm 56–60, for example). This psalm begins with an expression of the need for safety and refuge in this arena of anticipated death or loss. On the basis of language and content, other scholars (Ewald, for example[7]) place this psalm in the time of the Babylonian exile.[8] Possibly David wrote the initial psalm and it was edited later. It doesn't really matter too much. This is a psalm written by someone who senses the fragility of life, cries out for refuge, and finds it.

One year after my loss, I preached in my home church on the theme of grief and loss from this psalm. I only realized afterward that John Stek had described this as a psalm for safekeeping in the midst of death.[9] That made great sense of why I had found such strength from reading it during my time of acute grief. Death certainly seems to be the underlying reality to which verses 9–11 speak. The dilemma is resolved ultimately in the resurrection of Christ, and therefore in hope for all of the people of God

7. Ewald, *Commentary on the Psalms*, 15.

8. One of the major reasons these authors opt for this judgment is the clear articulation of resurrection in the latter verses, a doctrine they say does not appear in the OT in pre-exilic times. Delitzsch, however—though he admits the resurrection does not appear in pre-exilic times—postulates that there is no reason why it should not appear in Davidic psalms as "a bold postulate of faith." Cheyne's suggestion that this psalm presents the antithesis between life and God and life without God, and not this world and the next, flies in the face of NT interpretation of the psalm.

9. Stek, Psalms commentary in *NIV Study Bible*, 799.

in Christ.[10] The psalm also speaks plainly of the *"sorrows"* (v. 4) that characterize human life in a fallen creation in which death has not yet been destroyed. It acknowledges that these "sorrows"—which are the lot of all people, including the godly—can be "multiplied" by avoidance or pursuit of the idols and broken cisterns, which promise quick relief but never deliver. The assumption of the author of Psalm 16 is that we can not only face and experience our emotions, but that we can run to God with them in prayer. Good grief counseling has as its motto that we must go *through* grief, not around it. Psalm 16 is in agreement.

Verses 9–11 reassure us that death is not the final word. They speak of a continuance of the body, which, even when it dies, will rest secure (v. 9) and be accompanied by divine presence in death (v. 10), and then will be resurrected (v. 11). In an eternal state we share the enjoyment of the divine presence and life and joy (v. 11). These verses reassure me that death, even if only anticipated, *is* the key issue of the psalm, its most specific danger, the occasion of the most specific need for refuge, and the specific problem solved in the final verses.

When Peter preaches using Psalm 16:9–11 in his Pentecostal sermon, he makes the case that Psalm 16 could not have been fulfilled in David, for he was dead and his tomb was visible in Jerusalem at that time. Peter here demonstrates that the ultimate meaning and fulfillment of this psalm is christological. After Pentecost, the apostles would go on to develop the doctrine that because Christ had conquered death and was risen, so all in Christ would experience resurrection too. All in the new redeemed humanity, all in the last Adam, would be raised. In retrospect, this would include David too, as an Old Testament saint and a part of the covenant people of God. He was among the people of God in Christ retrospectively, even as we who came after the cross are in Christ prospectively. It is my suspicion that David saw this by faith when he wrote Psalm 16, but I have no direct evidence of this.

The New Testament usage of verses 9–11 for the death and resurrection of Jesus, David's greater Son and Lord, confirm that the final resolution of death is tied up in the death, resurrection, ascension, and second coming of Christ at the last resurrection. His death has destroyed death in order to take away its sting and our fear. Yet the full destruction accomplished at the cross and by the resurrection will not be fully applied until the second coming of Christ. In the "in between" time it is still "an enemy" (1 Cor 15:26),

---

10. See Acts 2:25–28; 13:35 where these verses in Psalm 16 are so interpreted.

and our encounters with it affect us profoundly. Whatever circumstances may assail the follower of Jesus, comfort can be gained from this psalm.

This psalm sets the story of our encounter with death within the larger setting of the Big Story of God's work in the world. This Big Story provides the frame we need as we struggle with loss and grief in all of our little stories. Here we find redemption for grief and resurrection hope for death.

This is the kind of message I have obtained from the Psalms, but not all encounters with a psalm are this grand. I have found it helpful to pray using the very words or my own impromptu translation of a psalm, and in doing so, to try to enter into all the emotions of the psalmist, without fear that I will displease God. These can include sadness, anger, anguish, regret, repentance, and on into joy.

Solitude

A second practice I have found helpful is solitude, which usually comes along with silence. I am by personality just as comfortable alone as I am with people, and just as glad for the one as for the other when the one is too long or intense. I had a great deal of alone when I first lost Sharon. My daughter Heather was vigilant and self-sacrificing to make sure I wasn't alone too much. However, times alone were necessary as the grief journey progressed, mainly because it is easy to cover up the deeper movements of the soul with activity and distraction, even work of a spiritual kind. In this I resonate very much with what Ruth Haley Barton writes concerning her early struggles with solitude. She writes of solitude as the "single most meaningful aspect of my spiritual life to date," but acknowledges the initial struggle:

> On the other hand, solitude and silence represent a continuing challenge for me. Though it has been well over ten years since I first said yes to God's invitation to enter more intentionally into these disciplines, I still find it challenging to protect space for these times apart which satisfy the deep empty places of my soul. Like you, I wrestle with the influences of the secular culture and even religious subcultures that in overt or subtle ways devalue non-productive times for being rather than doing. And I struggle to trust myself to the mystery that is God in the silent places beyond all the things I think I should know. By now I know better than to blame my struggle on forces "out there." I am more aware than ever that I have my own inner demons that are easily enticed—demons of

desire to perform, to be seen as competent (at least!), productive, culturally relevant, balanced. I still battle these demons. . . . But what a delight to keep experiencing God's invitations amidst the challenges!

Haley Barton then serves us by defining what solitude and silence really are:

> It is an invitation to enter more deeply into the intimacy of re-lationship with the One who waits just outside the noise and busyness of our lives. It is an invitation to communication and communion with the One who is always present even when our awareness has been dulled by distraction. It is an invitation to the adventure of spiritual transformation in the deepest places of our being, an adventure that will result in greater freedom and authen-ticity and surrender to God than we have yet experienced.[11]

I have found that seasons of intense difficulty and loss take us to a place of great spiritual and emotional softness and sensitivity to the pres-ence of the Lord. My season of intense depression in my thirties, and my loss of Sharon in my fifties, were of this nature. However, there was also that pull of the busy world of activity and achievement, or just the need to look okay, that threatened to close down the softness and sensitivity. Disciplin-ing my life to experience the silence is still required to maintain the sense of the Presence on a daily basis, and I have also been able to retreat often to our home on an island to recover it. It is not just that in the solitude and silence, one can feel the feelings and order the thoughts and affections. It is encountering Christ that transcends all this, and he does the ordering. For through all our sorrows and griefs, it is to him that we go. That's where broken hearts go! And he never fails. He is the same yesterday and today and forever.

---

11. Barton, *Invitation to Solitude and Silence*, 15–16. For one of the most helpful and grace-oriented treatments of the other spiritual disciplines, see by the same author, *Sa-cred Rhythms: Arranging Our Lives for Spiritual Transformation*.

Bibliography

Ainsworth, M. D., et al. *Patterns of Attachment: A Psychological Study of the Strange Situation*. Hillsdale, NJ: Erlbaum, 1978.

Anderson, Ray S. *On Being Human: Essays on Anthropology*. Pasadena, CA: Fuller Seminary Press, 1982.

Attig, Thomas. *How We Grieve: Relearning the World*. New York: Oxford University Press, 1996.

Autton, Norman. *The Pastoral Care of the Dying*. London: SPCK, 1966.

Balk, David E. "Grief Counseling without the Grief: A Readable Text for Beginning Counselors" (A Review of *Principles and Practice of Grief Counseling* by Howard R. Winokuer and Darcy L. Harris). *Death Studies* 38 (2014) 346–48.

Barber, P. *Becoming a Practitioner/Researcher: A Gestalt Approach to Holistic Inquiry*. Oxford: Libri, 2006.

Barth, Karl. *The Christian Life. Church Dogmatics* IV/4: Lecture Fragments. Translated by Geoffrey W. Bromiley. Reprint. Grand Rapids: Eerdmans, 1981.

———. *Church Dogmatics*. 14 vols. Edited by G. W. Bromiley and T. F. Torrance. 2nd ed. Edinburgh: T. & T. Clark, 1936–77.

Bartholomew K., and P. Shaver. "Methods of Assessing Adult Attachment: Do They Converge?" In *Attachment Theory and Close Relationships*, edited by J. A Simpson and S. W. Rholes, 25–45. New York: Guilford, 1998.

Barton, Ruth Haley. *Invitation to Solitude and Silence: Experiencing God's Transforming Presence*. Downers Grove, IL: IVP, 2010.

———. *Sacred Rhythms: Arranging Our Lives for Spiritual Transformation*. Downers Grove, IL: IVP, 2006.

Berkhof, Hendrikus. *Christian Faith: An Introduction to the Study of Faith*. Translated by Sierd Woudstra. Grand Rapids: Eerdmans, 1979.

Boerner, K., C. B. Wortman, and G. A. Bonanno. "Resilient or at Risk? A 4-Year Study of Older Adults Who Initially Showed High or Low Distress Following Conjugal Loss." *The Journals of Gerontology Series B: Psychological Sciences and Social Sciences* 60 (2005) 67–73.

Bonanno, George A. "Loss, Trauma, and Human Resilience: Have We Underestimated the Human Capacity to Thrive after Extremely Aversive Events?" *American Psychologist* 59 1 (2004) 20–28.

Bonanno, George A., et al. "Resilience to Loss and Chronic Grief: A Prospective Study from Pre-loss to 18 Months Post-Loss." *Journal of Personality and Social Psychology* 83.5 (2002) 1150–64.

Bowlby, John. *Attachment*. Attachment and Loss, 1. New York: Basic, 1980.

——. *Loss*. Attachment and Loss, 3. New York: Basic, 1980.

——. *The Making and Breaking of Affectional Bonds*. London: Tavistock, 1979.

——. *A Secure Base: Parent-Child Attachment and Healthy Human Development*. New York: Basic, 1988.

——. *Separation*. Attachment and Loss, 2. New York: Basic, 1973.

Brandon, L. Lawrence. *Treasures in the Darkness: Letting Go of Pain, Holding on to Faith*. Nashville, TN: Abingdon, 2013.

Bretherton, Luke. *Hospitality as Holiness: Christian Witness amid Moral Diversity*. Aldershot, UK: Ashgate, 2006.

Bruce, F. F. *The New Testament Documents: Are They Reliable?* 6th ed. Grand Rapids: Eerdmans, 2003.

Brueggemann, Walter. "The Formfulness of Grief." In Atla Serials, https://korycapps.files. wordpress.com/2012/11/w-brueggemann_-the-formfulness-of-grief.pdf.

Buber, Martin. *The Knowledge of Man*. London: Allen and Unwin, 1965.

Calvin, John. *Institutes of the Christian Religion*, 1559, 1–2. Translated by Ford Lewis Battles, edited by John T. McNeill. The Library of Christian Classics, 20–21. Philadelphia: Westminster, 1960.

John Calvin, "How Christ Is the Mediator: A Response to the Polish Brethren to Refute Stancaro's Error." Translated by Joseph N. Tylenda, in "Christ the Mediator: Calvin versus Stancaro," by Joseph N. Tylenda. *Calvin Theological Journal* 8.1 (1973) 11–16.

Canlis, Julie. *Calvin's Ladder: A Spiritual Theology of Ascent and Ascension*. Grand Rapids: Eerdmans, 2010.

Carhart-Harris, Robin L., et al. "Mourning and Melancholia Revisited: Correspondences between Principles of Freudian Metapsychology and Empirical Findings in Neuropsychiatry." *Annals of General Psychiatry* 7.9 (2008) 1–23.

Catherine of Siena. *The Dialogue*. Classics of Western Spirituality. New York: Paulist, 1980.

Center, C. *Grief and Loss*, 2007. www.counselingcenter.illinois.edu.

Clewell, Tammy. "Mourning Beyond Melancholia: Freud's Psychoanalysis of Loss." *J. Am. Psychoanal. Assoc.* 52 (2004) 43–67.

Crabb, Larry. *Connecting: Healing Ourselves and Our Relationships*. Nashville, TN: Thomas Nelson, 2005.

Cunningham, David. *These Three Are One: The Practice of Trinitarian Theology*. Oxford: Blackwell, 1998.

Currier, Joseph M., Jason M. Holland, and Robert A. Neimeyer. "Sense-Making, Grief, and the Experience of Violent Loss: Toward a Mediational Model." *Death Studies* 30 (2006) 403–28.

Currier, Joseph M., et al. "Bereavement, Religion, and Posttraumatic Growth: A Matched Control Group Investigation." *Psychology of Religion and Spirituality* 5.2 (2013) 69–77.

Currier, J. M., R. A. Neimeyer, and J. S. Berman. "The Effectiveness of Psychotherapeutic Interventions for the Bereaved: A Comprehensive Quantitative Review." *Psychological Bulletin*, 134 (2008) 648–61.

Delitzsch, Franz. *A Commentary on the Book of Psalms*, 1. Translated by David Eaton and James Duguid. New York: Funk and Wagnalls, 1883.

Derrida, Jacques. *The Work of Mourning*. Translated by Pascale-Anne Brault and Michael Naas. Chicago: University of Chicago Press, 2001.

Doka, Kenneth J., and Amy S. Tucci, eds. *Beyond Kübler-Ross: New Perspectives on Death, Dying and Grief.* Washington, DC: Hospice Foundation of America, 2011.

Doka, Kenneth J. ed. *Living with grief: Before and After the Death.* Washington, DC: Hospice Foundation of America, 2007.

Eadie, John. *Commentary on the Epistle of Paul to the Ephesians.* Minneapolis: James and Klock Christian, 1977.

Egan, G. *The Skilled Helper.* 4th ed. Pacific Grove, CA: Brooks/Cole, 1990.

Ellithorpe, Anne-Marie. "Teresa of Avila and Authentic Friendship." Paper presented at AAR/SBL/ASOR Pacific Northwest Region, Portland, Oregon, March 17, 2013.

Ewald, G. Heinrich. *A v Commentary on the Psalms.* Translated by E. Johnson. Commentary on the Poetical Books of the Old Testament 1. London: Williams and Norgate, 1880–81.

Fiddes, Paul S. *The Creative Suffering of God.* Oxford: Clarendon, 1988.

Fishman, Alyssa. "Grief Counseling without the Grief: A Readable Text for Beginning Counselors." *Death Studies* 38.5 (2013) 346–48.

Friedman, M. "Reflections on the Buber-Rogers Debate." *Journal of Humanistic Psychology* 34 (1994) 46–65.

Freud, Sigmund. "Mourning and Melancholia." In *The Standard Edition of the Complete Psychological Works of Sigmund Freud,* xiv. Translated by James Strachey, 239–60. London: Hogarth, 1914–16.

Grenz, Stanley J., and Roy D. Bell. *Betrayal of Trust: Confronting and Preventing Clergy Sexual Misconduct.* 2nd ed. Grand Rapids: Baker, 2001.

Gunton, Colin. *The Promise of Trinitarian Theology.* 2nd ed. London: T. & T. Clark/ Bloomsbury, 1997.

Hastings, William Ross. *The Life of God in Jonathan Edwards: Towards an Evangelical Theology of Participation.* Minneapolis: Fortress, 2015.

———. *Missional God, Missional Church: Hope for Re-evangelizing the West.* Downers Grove, IL: IVP Academic, 2012.

Haugk, Kenneth C. *Don't Sing Songs to a Heavy Heart: How to Relate to Those Who Are Suffering.* St. Louis, MO: Stephen Ministries, 2004.

Hinton, Clara. *Silent Grief.* Green Forest, AZ: New Leaf, 1997.

Holland, Jason M., and Robert A. Neimeyer. "Reducing the Risk of Burnout in End-of-Life Care Settings: The Role of Daily Spiritual Experiences and Training." *Palliative & Supportive Care* 3 (2005) 173–81.

Holmes, Stephen R. *The Quest for the Trinity: The Doctrine of God in Scripture, History and Modernity.* Downers Grove, IL: IVP Academic, 2012.

Holmes, Thomas H., and Richard H. Rahe. "The Social Readjustment Rating Scale." *Journal of Psychosomatic Research* II (1967) 213–18.

Houston, James. *The Transforming Friendship.* 1991. Reprint. Carol Stream, IL: NavPress, 1996.

———. Lectures in "Trinitarian Spirituality." Unpublished. Regent College, 1989.

Hunsinger, George. "The Bread That We Break: Toward a Chalcedonian Resolution of the Eucharistic Controversies." *The Princeton Seminary Bulletin* XXIV.2 (2003) 241–58.

Johnson, Sue. *Hold Me Tight: Seven Conversations for a Lifetime of Love.* New York: Little, Brown and Company, 2008.

Joseph, Stephen, and P. Alex Linley. "Positive Adjustment to Threatening Events: An Organismic Valuing Theory of Growth through Adversity." *Review of General Psychology* 9 (2005) 262–80.

Kaplan, H., B. Sadock, and J. Grebb. *Kaplan and Sadock's Synopsis of Psychiatry*. 7th ed. Baltimore, MD: Williams and Wilkins, 1994.

Kelley, Melissa. *Grief: Contemporary Theory and the Practice of Ministry*. Minneapolis: Fortress, 2010.

Kirkpatrick, Lee. *Attachment, Evolution and the Psychology of Religion*. New York: Guilford, 2005.

———. "Attachment and Religious Representations and Behavior." In *Handbook of Attachment: Theory, Research and Clinical Applications*, edited by J. Cassidy and P. R. Shaver, 803–22. New York: Guilford, 1999.

Kirschenbaum, H., and V. Land Henderson, eds. *The Carl Rogers Reader*. London: Constable, 1990.

Koenig, Harold G., Kenneth I. Pargament, and Julie Nielsen. "Religious Coping and Health Status in Medically Ill Hospitalized Older Adults." *The Journal of Nervous & Mental Disease* 186 (1998) 513–21.

Konigsberg, Ruth Davis. "New Ways to Think about Grief." *TIME*, January 29, 2011, 1–4. http://content.time.com/time/magazine/article/0,9171,2042372-1,00.html.

———. *The Truth about Grief: The Myth of Its Five Stages and the New Science of Loss*. New York: Simon & Schuster, 2011.

Krupnick, Janice L. "Bereavement during Childhood and Adolescence." In *Bereavement: Reactions, Consequences, and Care*, edited by M. Osterweis, F. Solomon and M. Green, 97–142. Washington, DC: National Academies Press (US), 1984.

Krantzler, Mel. *Creative Divorce*. New York: New American Library, Signet, 1973.

Larson, Dale G. "Taking Stock: Past Contributions and Current Thinking on Death, Dying, and Grief." *Death Studies* 38.5 (2014) 349–52.

Laurie, Anna, and Robert A. Neimeyer. "African Americans in Bereavement: Grief as a Function of Ethnicity." *OMEGA—Journal of Death and Dying* 57 (2008) 173–93.

Lazar, Aryeh, and Jeffrey P. Bjorck. "Religious Support and Psychosocial Well-being among a Religious Jewish Population." *Mental Health, Religion & Culture* 11 (2008) 403–21.

Lennox, John. *God's Undertaker: Has Science Buried God?* Oxford: Lion, 2009.

Lewis, C. S. *The Great Divorce*. 1961. Reprint. New York: Harper Collins, 2009.

———. *A Grief Observed*. 1961. Reprint. New York: Harper Collins, 2009.

Lindemann, E. "Symptomatology and Management of Acute Grief." *American Journal of Psychiatry AJP* (1944) 141–48.

Lussier, Martine. "'Mourning and Melancholia': The Genesis of a Text and of a Concept." *International Journal of Psychoanalysis* 81 (2000) 667–86.

Martz, Erin, and Hanoch Livneh, eds. *Coping with Chronic Illness and Disability: Theoretical, Empirical, and Clinical Aspects*. New York: Springer, 2007.

McCormack, Bruce. *Karl Barth's Critically Realistic Dialectical Theology: Its Genesis and Development 1909–1936*. Oxford: Oxford University Press, 1995.

McFadyen, Alistair. *The Call to Personhood: The Christian Theory of the Individual*. Cambridge: Cambridge University Press, 1993.

———. "The Trinity and Human Individuality: The Conditions For Relevance." *Theology* 95 (1992) 10–18.

Mitsch, Ray, and Lynn Brookside. *Grieving the Loss of Someone You Love: Daily Meditations to Help You through the Grieving Process*. Ann Arbor, MI: Vine, 1993.

Moltmann, Jürgen. *The Crucified God: The Cross of Christ as the Foundation and Criticism of Christian Theology*. Minneapolis: Fortress, 1993.

———. *God in Creation. (The Gifford Lectures, 1984–1985)*. Minneapolis: Fortress, 1993.

———. *The Trinity and the Kingdom*. San Francisco: Harper & Row, 1981.

Moule, Handley C. G. *Studies In Ephesians*. Grand Rapids: Kregel, 1977.

Murphree, Jon Tal. *The Trinity and Human Personality: God's Model for Relationships*. Nappanee, IN: Evangel, 2001.

Neimeyer, R. A., H. G. Prigerson, and B. Davies. "Mourning and Meaning." *American Behavioral Scientist* 46.2 (2002) 235–51.

Neimeyer, Robert A., and D. C. Sands. "Meaning Reconstruction in Bereavement: From Principles to Practice." In *Grief and Bereavement in Contemporary Society Bridging Research and Practice*, edited by R. A. Neimeyer, D. L. Harris, H. R. Winokuer, and Gordon F. Thornton, 9–22. New York: Routledge, 2011.

Neimeyer, Robert A. *Grief and Bereavement in Contemporary Society: Bridging Research and Practice*. New York: Routledge, 2011.

———. *Meaning Reconstruction and the Experience of Loss*. Washington, DC: American Psychological Association, 2001.

———. "Narrative Strategies in Grief Therapy." *Journal of Constructivist Psychology* 12 (1999) 65–85.

Neuhaus, Richard John, ed. *The Eternal Pity: Reflections on Dying*. Notre Dame, IN: University of Notre Dame Press, 2000.

Newbigin, Lesslie. "The Trinity as Public Truth." In *The Trinity in a Pluralistic Age*, edited by Kevin Vanhoozer, 1–8. Grand Rapids: Eerdmans, 1997.

Nouwen, Henri. *Bread for the Journey: A Daybook of Wisdom and Faith*. Reprint. New York: HarperCollins, 2006.

Oden, Thomas. *Pastoral Theology: Essentials of Ministry*. San Francisco: HarperOne, 1983.

O'Donovan, Oliver. *Resurrection and the Moral Order*. 2nd ed. Leicester, UK: Apollos, 1994.

Osterweis M., Solomon F., and Green M., eds. *Bereavement: Reactions, Consequences, and Care*. Washington, DC: National Academies Press (US), 1984. (Chapter 5 is found at http://www.ncbi.nlm.nih.gov/books/NBK217842/)

Packer, J. I., and Richard Baxter. *A Grief Sanctified: Passing through Grief to Peace and Joy*. Ann Arbor, MI: Vine, 1997.

Pannenberg, Wolfhart. *Anthropology in Theological Perspective*. Philadelphia, Pennsylvania: Westminster, 1985.

———. *Basic Questions in Theology 1–2*. Translated by G. H. Kehn. London: SCM, 1970.

———. "The Reconciling Power of the Trinity." Geneva Conference of European Churches, C.E.C. Occasional Paper 15. Geneva: C.E.C., 1983.

Pargament, Kenneth I., Harold G. Koenig, and Lisa M. Perez. "The Many Methods of Religious Coping: Development and Initial Validation of the RCOPE." *Journal of Clinical Psychology* 56 (2000) 519–43.

Pargament, Kenneth I. *The Psychology of Religion and Coping: Theory, Research, Practice*. New York: Guilford, 1997.

Parkes, Colin Murray. *Bereavement*. New York: International Universities Press, 1972.

Pembroke, Neil. "Space in the Trinity and Pastoral Care." *Journal of Pastoral Care and Counselling* 65.2 (2011) 3.1–10.

Pinnock, Clark. *Set Forth Your Case: Studies in Christian Apologetics*. Nutley, NJ: Craig, 1968.

Polanyi, Michael. *The Tacit Dimension*. New York: Doubleday, 1966.

Plantinga, Cornelius. *Not the Way It's Supposed to Be: A Breviary of Sin*. Reprint. Grand Rapids: Eerdmans, 1999.

———. "The Threeness/Oneness Problem of the Trinity." *Calvin Theological Journal* 23 (1988) 37–53.

Polkinghorne, John. *Science and the Trinity: the Christian Encounter with Reality*. New Haven: Yale University Press, 2004.

Price, Daniel J. "Issues Related to Human Nature, Discovering a Dynamic Concept of the Person in Both Psychology and Theology." *Perspectives on Science and Christian Faith* 45 (1993) 170–80. The American Science Affiliation: http://www.asa3.org/ASA/PSCF/1993/PSCF9-93Price.html.

———. *Karl Barth's Anthropology in Light of Modern Thought*. Grand Rapids: Eerdmans, 2002.

Purves, Andrew. *Reconstructing Pastoral Theology: A Christological Foundation*. Louisville, KY: Westminster John Knox, 2004.

Roberts, Justin M. *Behold Our God: Contemplative Theology for the Soul*. Eugene, OR: Wipf and Stock, 2014.

Rohr, Richard. "An Appetite for Wholeness: Living with Our Sexuality." *Sojourners*, November 1982, 30.

Rogers, Carl. "The Necessary and Sufficient Conditions of Therapeutic Personality Change." In *The Carl Rogers Reader*, edited by H. Kirschenbaum and V. Land Henderson, 219–35. London: Constable, 1990.

Roos, Susan. "Chronic Sorrow and Ambiguous Loss: Gestalt Methods for Coping with Grief." *Gestalt Review* 17.3 (2013) 229–39.

Roos, Susan, and Robert A. Neimeyer. "Reauthoring the Self: Chronic Sorrow and Posttraumatic Stress Following the Onset of CID." In *Coping with Chronic Illness and Disability: Theoretical, Empirical, and Clinical Aspects*, edited by Erin Martz and Hanoch Livneh, 89–106. New York: Springer, 2007.

Ross, Ellen M. *The Grief of God Images of the Suffering Jesus in Late Medieval England*. New York: Oxford University Press, 1997.

Saliers, Don, E. ed. *Prayer: Barth*. 50th anniversary ed. Louisville, KY: Westminster John Knox, 2002.

Schwöbel, Christoph, ed. *Trinitarian Theology Today*. Edinburgh: T. & T. Clark, 1995.

Schwöbel, Christoph, and Colin Gunton, eds. *Persons Divine and Human*. Edinburgh: T. & T. Clark, 1991.

Shepherd, Andrew, and Steven Prediger. *The Gift of the Other: Levinas, Derrida, and a Theology of Hospitality*. Eugene, OR: Pickwick, 2014.

Schmemann, Alexander. *For the Life of the World: Sacraments and Orthodoxy*. 2nd ed. Crestwood, NY: St. Vladimir's Seminary Press, 1973.

Simpson, J. A., and S. W. Rholes, eds. *Attachment Theory and Close Relationships*. New York: Guilford, 1998.

Sittser, Gerald Lawson. *A Grace Disguised: How the Soul Grows through Loss*. Grand Rapids: Zondervan, 1996.

Smit, Laura. "Developing a Calvinist Sacramental Theology." Calvin Institute of Worship. http://www.calvin.edu/worship/idis/theol9ogy/sacraments/calvinist.php.

Smith, C. "Unit 1 Live Session [Power point slides]," 2012. www.breeze.careeredonline.com/p559890471/.

Smith, Wilbur M. *Therefore Stand: Christian Apologetics*. Grand Rapids: Baker, 1965.

Stek, John H. Psalms commentary in the *NIV Study Bible*, New International Version. Grand Rapids: Zondervan, 2002.

Stevens, R. Paul. *Disciplines of a Hungry Heart: Christian Living Seven Days a Week.* Wheaton, IL: Shaw, 1993.

Stix, Gary. "The Neuroscience of True Grit." *Scientific American* 304, March 2011, 28–33.

Stroebe, M. S., et al., eds. *Handbook of Bereavement Research and Practice: Advances in Theory and Intervention.* Washington, DC: American Psychological Association, 2008.

Sullender, R. Scott. *Grief and Growth: Pastoral Resources for Emotional and Spiritual Growth.* Mahwah, NJ: Paulist, 1985.

———. "Grief's Multi-dimensional Nature: A Review of Melissa M. Kelley's Grief: Contemporary Theory and the Practice of Ministry." *Pastoral Psychol* 63 (2014) 113.

Sullivan, Harry Stack, ed. *The Interpersonal Theory of Psychiatry.* New York: Norton, 1953.

———. *The Collected Works of Harry Stack Sullivan.* 2 vols. New York: Norton, 1953, 1956.

Sunderland, Ronald. *Getting through Grief: Caregiving by Congregations.* Nashville, TN: Abingdon, 1993.

Switzer, David K. *The Dynamics of Grief.* Nashville, TN: Abingdon, 1970.

Taylor, Jeremy. *The Whole Works; with an Essay Biographical and Critical* 1. London: Westley and Davis, 1835.

Teresa of Avila. *Book of Her Life.* The Collected Works of St. Teresa of Avila. Washington, DC: ICS, 1987.

———. *The Way of Perfection.* Translated and edited by E. Allison Peers. Garden City, NJ: Doubleday, 1991.

Torrance, Alan. "On Deriving Ought from Is: Christology, Covenant and *Koinonia*." In *The Doctrine of God and Theological Ethics*, edited by Alan Torrance and Michael Banner, 167–190. Edinburgh: T. & T. Clark, 2006.

———. *Persons in Communion: Essay on Trinitarian Description and Human Participation.* Edinburgh: T. & T. Clark, 1996.

Torrance, James B. *Worship, Community and The Triune God of Grace.* Downers Grove, IL: IVP, 1996.

Torrance, T. F. *Calvin's Doctrine of Man.* Grand Rapids: Eerdmans, 1957.

———. *Reality and Evangelical Theology.* Philadelphia: Westminster, 1982.

Van Inwagen, Peter. "And Yet They are Not Three Gods But One God." In *Philosophy and the Christian Faith*, edited by Thomas V. Morris, 241–78. Notre Dame, IN: University of Notre Dame Press, 1988.

Vanhoozer, Kevin, ed. *The Trinity in a Pluralistic Age: Theological Essays on Culture and Religion.* Grand Rapids: Eerdmans, 1997.

Volf, Miroslav. *After Our Likeness: The Church as the Image of the Trinity.* Grand Rapids: Eerdmans, 1998.

Wen, Clement Yung. "The Monergistic Theme of Participation in the Anthropological Soteriology of John Calvin: A Dialogue with Maximus the Confessor." Master of Christian Studies thesis, Regent College, 2011.

Westberg, Granger E. *Good Grief.* Philadelphia: Fortress, 1962.

Williams, Rowan. *Teresa of Avila.* 1991. Reprint. London: Continuum, 2002.

Williams, Stephen. "The Trinity and Other Religions." In *The Trinity in a Pluralistic Age: Theological Essays on Culture and Religion*, edited by Kevin Vanhoozer, 26–40. Grand Rapids: Eerdmans, 1997.

Winokuer, Howard Robin, and Darcy Harris. *Principles and Practice of Grief Counseling.* New York: Springer, 2012.

Witvliet, John D. "The Doctrine of the Trinity and the Theology and Practice of Christian Worship in the Reformed Tradition." PhD diss., Notre Dame, 1997.

Wolterstorff, Nicholas. *Lament for a Son.* Grand Rapids: Eerdmans, 1987.

Worden, J. William. *Grief Counseling and Grief Therapy: A Handbook for the Mental Health Practitioner.* 4th ed. New York: Springer, 2009.

Wright, N. T. *The New Testament and the People of God.* Minneapolis: Fortress, 1992.

———. *Surprised by Hope: Rethinking Heaven, the Resurrection, and the Mission of the Church.* New York: HarperOne, 2008.

Zunin, Leonard M., and Hilary Stanton Zunin. *The Art of Condolence: What to Write, What to Say, What to Do at a Time of Loss.* New York: HarperCollins, 1991.

Zylla, Phillip Charles. *The Roots of Sorrow: A Pastoral Theology of Suffering.* Waco, TX: Baylor University Press, 2012.

Name/Subject Index

analogy of being (*analogia entis*), 50n6, 62
analogy of relations (*analogia relationis*), 50n6, 55, 62, 73
Anderson, Ray, 57
Anselm, 38
Attachment Theory, ix, 12, 19, 46, 62, 71, 73, 74, 74n25, 87
Augustine, 38, 47

Barber, Paul, 78
Barth, Karl, 50n6, 52n13, 53, 62, 73, 90
Barton, Ruth Haley, 143–44
Bell, Roy, 58
Berkhof, Hendrikus, 52n13
Bhaskar, Roy, 38
Boersma, Hans, 119
Boethius, 54, 56
Bonanno, George, 133–35
Brandon, L. Lawrence, 35n11
bridging concepts, 50–53
Bruce, F.F., 40n7
Brueggeman, Walter, 4, 140
Buber, Martin, 122, 126–27

Calvin, John, 19, 51–52, 139
camouflaged grief, 79, 80
Canlis, Julie, 52
Cappadocians, the, 47n1, 54, 122
Catherine of Siena, 90, 91n4
Chalcedonian, 55–56
Churchill, Winston, 103
Clemens, Samuel, 22

Clewell, Tammy, 71
Cognitive Behavioral School, 71
coinherence, 49, 90, 92, 122
compatibilism, asymmetric 91
counseling, 124–30
Crabb, Larry, 115
Cunningham, David, 122

deconstruction, 78, 81–83
defence mechanisms, 22, 29, 65, 67, 68, 71
denial, 22, 68, 80, 81, 82n3, 127, 131, 135, 136
depression, 30–35, 58, 60, 71, 79, 128, 136
Derrida, Jacques, 71, 74
divorce, 2, 12, 14, 87

Eade, John, 94n8
Eastern Orthodox Church, 41, 111
Edwards, Jonathan, 47n1, 62n3
Egan, G., 124
Ellithorpe, Anne-Marie, 116–17
equiprimal, 47
eucharist, 114, 114n3, 138–40

Fairbairn, R.D.W., 19, 42, 69, 70, 73
Farmer, Richard Allen, 33
fatigue, 93
Freud, Sigmund, 42–44, 69–73, 133
funerals, 82, 83, 120, 131

gestalt, 78, 79
Gorer, Geoffrey, 14

153

Scripture index

Made in the USA
San Bernardino, CA
09 January 2018